The Dell Guides for Mental Health

Why Does Everything Have to Be Perfect?

Understanding Obsessive-Compulsive Disorder

Lynn Schackman, M.D.
and
Shelagh Ryan Masline

A Dell Mental Health Guide
Series Editor: Roger Granet, M.D.

A DELL BOOK

Published by
Dell Publishing
a division of
Random House, Inc.
1540 Broadway
New York, New York 10036

Dell books may be purchased for business or promotional use or for special sales. For information please write to: Special Markets Department, Random House, Inc., 1540 Broadway, New York, NY 10036.

Dell® is a registered trademark of Random House, Inc., and the colophon is a trademark of Random House, Inc.

ISBN: 0-440-23463-8

Designed by Donna Sinisgalli

Printed in the United States of America

Published simultaneously in Canada

August 1999

10 9 8 7 6 5 4 3 2 1

OPM

Contents

Foreword

Pam, a nineteen-year-old college student, is studying for her final exams. But she is finding it increasingly difficult to concentrate. Everything she touches appears to be covered with germs, and every time she picks up a book or handles her class notes, she feels compelled to strenuously scrub her hands. As a result, her hands are now red and raw. In the hope of eliminating the germs, Pam takes many showers each day, often for hours on end. Although she is an intelligent woman who can appreciate that these concerns are inconsistent with what she knows intellectually, Pam is completely unable to alter her behavior. Sadly, but not surprisingly, these distractions and the many hours that she spends trying vainly to cope with the fears that plague her cause Pam's grades to slip, which further exacerbates her dilemma.

Frank, a man in his late fifties, cannot stop himself from hoarding every conceivable newspaper, catalog, and magazine that comes his way, even those that his neighbors discard. He is certain that they will be of value to him at a later date, but he does not even read most of what he saves. Over time his apartment, not large to begin with, becomes so cluttered and the piles grow so high that his family and friends are actually precluded from visiting. Eventually, after a neighbor complains of the fire hazard in his apartment, Frank is served with an eviction notice.

There are between five and six million men and women in the United States just like Pam and Frank. They suffer from this country's fourth most common psychiatric illness: obsessive-compulsive disorder, or OCD. OCD has long been unappreciated in its scope and frequency of occurrence. For many years, it was misdiagnosed or, worse, unrecognized, because its symptoms were kept hidden from view by people like Pam and Frank who wished to avoid embarrassment. Most people are astonished to learn how common OCD really is. When sufferers hear that they have a recognized illness, previously inexplicable behavior can be put into context and addressed in a meaningful way.

The following anecdote may bring this point home. About ten years ago, when I was a researcher at the Anxiety Disorders Program of the Payne-Whitney Clinic, the ABC News program 20/20 broadcast one of the very first reports describing OCD. The next day the phones at the clinic were flooded with callers, all saying basically the same thing. People were enormously relieved to discover that their obsession with germs or their compulsion to clean, check, or repeatedly do something were actually the symptoms of a biologically driven disease. For years they had kept their disorder a secret from even their closest loved ones. When they could reveal their problem and seek appropriate treatment, a great burden was lifted from their shoulders.

OCD is a disease of obsessions—unsettling thoughts, fears, and images that occur time and time again—and compulsions—repetitive behaviors that its sufferers are driven to perform in an attempt to alleviate extreme anxiety. OCD sufferers engage in visibly inappropriate and unusual conduct and often experience bizarre thoughts, but the distinguishing aspect of the illness is that they are themselves very much aware that these thoughts and behavior patterns are occurring and are at odds with their own understanding of normal behavior. Therefore people such as Pam and Frank are unable to share their doubts and fears with their family, their friends, or even their physicians.

The goal of this book is to identify these disturbing fears and rituals and examine the biological underpinnings of OCD. We will discuss, in addition, current treatments for this condition, which include medication with selective serotonin-reuptake inhibitors and behavior therapy.

The explosion of research into OCD during the past decade has led to increasingly refined and effective diagnosis and treatment. Many studies have focused on the role of serotonin, and others have used PET scanners to isolate particular parts of the brain that are active when OCD symptoms are present. Unfortunately, children have not been spared from this illness, as pediatric forms of OCD have been identified. Investigation into OCD is ongoing, and research scientists and practicing mental health professionals can claim only a partial understanding of all its complexities. As we enter the next millennium, however, further attention to OCD promises to result in even more effective means of treatment.

For Pam and Frank and all their affected peers, recognizing the signs and symptoms of OCD is helpful. Since OCD doesn't go away on its own, seeking professional assistance at the earliest possible time is far better than waiting until a crisis develops. Following treatment, OCD sufferers can control their uncomfortable anxiety-provoking thoughts and actions, thereby allowing for happier and healthier lives.

—Lynn Schackman, M.D.
November 1998

Chapter 1

OBSESSIVE-COMPULSIVE DISORDER: DEFINITIONS AND OVERVIEW

Obsessive-compulsive disorder, or OCD, is one of the most common but frequently underdiagnosed mental health problems of our time. Until very recently OCD—an anxiety disorder of overwhelming obsessions and repeated rituals that sufferers are powerless to stop—was considered rare and difficult to treat. Today we know that this disturbing and at times even incapacitating disease affects as many as one in forty people, making it the fourth most common of all psychiatric disorders. In the past ten years, we have also learned a great deal about coping with OCD, and the good news is that it is a highly treatable illness. Even though OCD will usually continue to cause some degree of distress to those afflicted with it, medication and behavior therapy can help control its symptoms and significantly improve the quality of life for OCD sufferers.

The signs of OCD are probably familiar to most of us, and you may very well have read about or seen or even met someone who suffers from this disorder. Long ago Shakespeare wrote of Lady Macbeth washing and rewashing her hands, trying in vain to remove the spot that only she could see. In the hit film *As Good As It Gets,* Jack Nicholson's character, obsessed with cleanliness and order, carefully steps over every crack in the sidewalk and insists on eating with his own plastic knife and fork when he visits a restaurant. And earlier this century, the reclusive multimillionaire Howard Hughes was famous for carefully sealing the doors and windows of his homes with paper towels and tissues to prevent errant germs from slipping in.

These were all rituals designed to relieve fears of contamination, a very common obsession in OCD. Yet while extreme behavior patterns such as these easily lend themselves to either tragic or humorous portrayal in literature and film, the reality is that they cause acute pain and distress to those suffering from them. People who have OCD are in fact fully aware of how bizarre and irrational their obsessions and compulsions may be, but without proper treatment they cannot control them and often go to extreme lengths to conceal them.

What is obsessive-compulsive disorder?

OCD is a common anxiety disorder characterized by upsetting and demanding thoughts and rituals that are virtually impossible to control. The unsettling thoughts or ideas are called obsessions; actions performed to reduce the distress caused by them are called compulsions. Usually both anxious thoughts and rituals are present, although in some cases it may be only one or the other. Obsessions and compulsions range in intensity from mildly interfering to extremely disabling. In contrast to those suffering from other psychiatric problems, people who have OCD are conscious of and commonly painfully embarrassed by the unusual thoughts and behavior that typify their disease.

What are obsessive thoughts like?

Thoughts grow increasingly uncomfortable and troubling to someone who has OCD. A perfectly healthy person may believe that he will catch a life-threatening illness just by touching a doorknob, or while driving down the road suddenly and without justification, he may become convinced that he has caused a terrible traffic accident. Many OCD sufferers are racked with doubt and guilt about simple things such as whether they left the stove on or the coffeemaker plugged in and might consequently cause a fire. Others have extremely disturbing thoughts of a violent, sexually inappropriate, or blasphemous nature.

What is the relationship between obsessions and compulsions?

When you have OCD, it is very difficult to get anguishing thoughts out of your mind. People may find relief from their obsessions only by engaging in compulsive, ritualistic behavior. And since that relief never lasts, they act out the rituals again and again. Sufferers eventually become locked into very rigid, absolute, and unforgiving patterns of thought and/or behavior.

There is often a direct link between obsessions and compulsions. The most common obsession by far is a fear of contamination by dirt, germs, or disease, and rituals typically used to relieve the resultant nervousness and apprehension are washing the hands until they are red and raw or showering for hours on end.

Checking is another very common type of compulsive behavior. "Checkers" are obsessed with doubt and guilt that they may harm others, and so they may repeatedly drive over the same patch of road to check that they have not caused an accident, or return home again and again to make certain that the stove and coffeemaker have been turned off.

When checking does not seem sufficient, some people also engage in "undoing" rituals, such as mentally counting or repeating a complicated string of numbers again and again to ward off some imagined disaster. Others are driven to hoard trivial objects, such as bits of string, old newspapers, and sometimes even trash. Many are preoccupied with symmetry and order, and they spend hours uselessly arranging paper clips in a drawer or shoes in the closet.

How do people with OCD feel about their disorder?

Most people with OCD suffer in silence and are slow in seeking medical treatment, since their behavior embarrasses, confuses, and frightens them. Even though they recognize that the irrational thoughts and rituals consuming their lives make no sense and at times try to resist or control them, the urges to carry them out are overwhelming.

Everyone calls me a perfectionist. Does that mean I have OCD?

Many people are perfectionists, who must have every little thing just right, but most of these people do not have OCD. A painstaking attention to detail and order, often a hallmark of OCD sufferers, is also a highly desirable trait shared by successful professionals, from doctors to editors to computer programmers. But these detail-oriented perfectionists are by and large a happy lot, content with and even proud of the meticulous habits that help them get ahead in the working world.

The person with OCD, on the other hand, is intensely ashamed of his thoughts and rituals and will go to great lengths to hide them. And while his thoroughness may at first glimpse appear to be an admirable trait, it rapidly becomes excessive and eventually interferes with his work. For example, the secretary who checks his own work once is efficient—but checking it ten or twenty or even thirty times is an increasingly inefficient waste of time. In sharp contrast to the fortunate perfectionist, the OCD sufferer experiences painful feelings of humiliation, discomfort, and loss of control as a result of his preoccupation with order and symmetry, and in severe cases he cannot even hold down a job.

How can I tell if I am suffering from this disorder?

Many healthy people can identify with some of the symptoms of OCD, such as checking once or twice to make sure the lights are turned off and the door is locked when leaving the house. Some of us may also believe in certain superstitions, such as knocking on wood or not crossing the path of a black cat. But people with OCD tend to take these notions to extremes. If you become overly concerned with these kinds of habits or beliefs and devote more than an hour a day to them—or if you find yourself spending an inordinate amount of time washing and cleaning, checking things, repeating thoughts or actions in an exact order, making sure that all the objects in your home or office are orderly and symmetrical, or experiencing recurring thoughts that you would like to get rid of but can't—you may be departing from the spectrum of normal behavior.

If you feel that your thoughts and habits are spiraling out of control and suspect that OCD might be the problem, three very important questions to ask yourself are:

1. Does obsessive-compulsive behavior consume an hour or more of my day?

2. Do intrusive thoughts and obsessions cause me severe distress, anxiety, guilt, or shame?

3. Do obsessions and compulsions significantly interfere with my day-to-day life?

If your answers to these questions are yes, you may be suffering from OCD. See your doctor and ask for a referral to a mental health professional who is trained and experienced in dealing with your problem. The good news is that medication and behavior therapy can help the vast majority of people with OCD minimize their afflictions and improve their quality of life.

Who develops obsessive-compulsive disorder?

OCD affects people of all ages and in all walks of life, and it appears in countries all around the world. Unlike most other anxiety disorders, which affect primarily women, OCD strikes men and women in equal numbers. On average, the disease first appears in the teens or early adulthood, and about a third of adults who have OCD initially experienced its symptoms as children. There is also some evidence indicating that OCD runs in families.

How common is OCD?

As many as one in every forty people you know or meet may be afflicted with OCD. While problems such as depression have long been recognized, until very recently OCD was considered to be a rare and exotic disease. In the last ten years a great deal has been learned about OCD, and now we know that it is the fourth most common psychiatric disorder in the United States, following only depression, substance abuse, and phobias. OCD affects roughly two and a half percent of the world's population, and in this country an estimated five to six million people suffer from the disorder.

What causes OCD?

While a stressful event such as a move or a job change may trigger an episode of OCD, its root cause is now widely believed to be biological rather than behavioral. Like the majority of psychiatric disorders, OCD is no longer attributed solely to life circumstances. Experts today believe that OCD is caused by a chemical imbalance of the neurotransmitter serotonin in the brain. Neurotransmitters are important chemicals that are released from nerve cells and carry messages to other cells in other parts of the brain.

How is OCD diagnosed?

Recurrent unwanted thoughts and/or ritualistic behavior of which a person is ashamed—and over which he has little or no control—lead to a diagnosis of OCD. Interestingly, there has traditionally been an enormous time lapse between the onset of OCD and its subsequent diagnosis and treatment. In fact, one study by Eric Hollander, M.D., et al, in 1996 indicated that an average of seventeen years passed between the appearance of the first symptoms and their appropriate treatment. Ten years of this period elapsed between the onset of symptoms and the seeking of professional help, followed by six years until the diagnosis was made, and an additional year and a half until proper treatment was given. This amazing gap was most likely due to a general lack of knowledge about the disease, as well as the fact that OCD sufferers tend to be ashamed of their problem and try to disguise its symptoms. As we come to a greater understanding of OCD, this time period can be dramatically shortened.

How do people with OCD usually react to their diagnosis?

Most people feel an enormous sense of relief when the diagnosis of OCD is finally made. It is hugely comforting to realize that they are not "crazy," that their symptoms are in fact the sign of a very specific and largely biochemical problem for which treatment can minimize its symptoms and help them to lead happier and healthier lives. With increasing awareness that OCD is an illness that is nobody's fault, it is hoped that more OCD sufferers will stop feeling that there is any shame or stigma attached to their ailment and will more promptly seek effective diagnosis and treatment.

What are the social costs of OCD?

Sadly, obsessions and compulsions prevent many OCD sufferers from living full and productive lives, and very often this illness leads to difficult interpersonal relationships both at home and on the job. True intimacy with a lover or spouse may elude those with OCD, who often feel compelled to cloak their obsessive thoughts and rituals in secrecy. Anger and resentment often follow the resultant lack of communication and understanding.

The hours consumed by obsessions and compulsions may also prevent a person with OCD from getting to work on time or from completing required tasks once he or she finally gets there. For example, some people with OCD take hours to shower and dress. They feel compelled to follow a certain very specific pattern—such as right sock first, not second—and if any variation occurs, they must repeat this rigid pattern from the very beginning. They may also have a preoccupation with symmetry. If their shoelaces are not tied exactly evenly or if their papers are not lined up just so on their desk, they must repeat the task again and again until they "get it right."

Not surprisingly, obsessive thoughts and compulsive habits consequently make it very difficult for the OCD sufferer to meet work or social obligations. Many think that people with OCD should "just get over it." Family members and co-workers alike may mistakenly believe that it is simply a matter of exercising one's will power. They do not take into account that letting go of obsessions and compulsions is in fact the OCD sufferer's fondest desire, but that in most circumstances it is impossible without proper treatment.

In very severe cases, preoccupation with fears and rituals can gradually become disabling, eating away at the structure of day-to-day existence, eroding marriage and family ties, destroying friendships, and ruining careers. OCD may eventually lead to an inability to have either a personal life or a job, as the entire day is taken up experiencing obsessive thoughts or performing rituals. Fortunately, more often than not OCD does not progress to these extremes.

Are there economic consequences to OCD?

OCD exacts a huge economic as well as emotional toll. A person with OCD generally loses three years of wages over the course of a lifetime. At an average yearly salary of $24,000, this amounts to some $47 billion in lost wages, a sizable drain on our country's economy.

The medical costs of OCD are also considerable. A recent survey conducted by the Obsessive Compulsive Foundation (OCF) found that 25 percent of respondents had been hospitalized. At an average cost of $12,500, the total lifetime hospital costs amounted to a substantial $5 billion. It is particularly unfortunate that a lack of knowledge about OCD often leads to many dollars spent on inappropriate care. In fact, experts estimate that cumulatively up to $2 billion a year is spent on unsuitable treatment.

What is the best treatment for OCD?

While over the years every possible remedy imaginable has been applied to OCD, only two have been shown to be effective: medication with serotonin-reuptake inhibitors and behavior therapy. Sometimes one or the other of these approaches works well separately, but in most cases a combination of the two is best. People with OCD also benefit by learning how to control stress, a common trigger of the disorder.

OCD appears to be due to a disturbance of serotonin activity in the brain, and therefore drugs that affect this neurotransmitter—serotonin-reuptake inhibitors—are far and away the most effective medication. These are Prozac (fluoxetine), Anafranil (clomipramine), Zoloft (sertraline), Luvox (fluvoxamine), and Paxil (paroxetine). If you don't respond to one of these medications, another may prove more beneficial to you. Treatment with tricyclic antidepressants (other than Anafranil) is generally not helpful, since OCD is specifically related to serotonin, not to other neurotransmitters such as norepinephrine or dopamine.

A type of behavior therapy known as exposure-and-response prevention has also proven very effective in treating OCD. Its goal is to stop unwanted behavior. The approach involves exposing someone to whatever stimulus triggers his problem, then helping him forgo the usual ritual. For example, a therapist might shake hands with a patient and then not allow him to wash his hands for five minutes. The next time he would be encouraged to wait ten minutes before washing, then twenty minutes, and so on. Although behavior therapy is helpful to many OCD sufferers, those who also suffer from depression may benefit from being on antidepressant medication to treat their underlying problem so that they can focus on therapy.

Are there other emotional aspects to OCD?

Not surprisingly, people who find themselves wasting hours a day on unwanted thoughts and rituals are apt to get depressed. In fact, some two-thirds of those suffering from OCD are diagnosed with depression. More than a third also have phobias, which are exaggerated and often disabling fears of objects or situations unrelated to any realistic danger. Other OCD sufferers are afflicted with eating disorders, and some use alcohol or drugs in a misguided attempt to control their symptoms. It's also common to experience OCD-related disorders, such as Tourette's syndrome, trichotillomania, body dysmorphic disorder, or autism. (Read more about these problems in Chapter 2.) In these cases, other treatment in addition to medication and behavior therapy is necessary.

How can my family help me cope with OCD?

Over time spouses and other family members often come to cope with the strain and frustration of living with an OCD sufferer by enabling him or her to act out rituals, and thus they unwittingly become coconspirators in allowing OCD behavior to occur. Because of this, treatment is usually most effective when the family is involved. It's very important for those close to you to realize that helping you to perform rituals only exaggerates and prolongs the self-destructive obsession-compulsion relationship that medication and therapy are intended to break.

Can obsessive-compulsive disorder be completely cured?

Unfortunately, OCD can never be completely cured. Although symptoms may wax and wane over the years, once you have OCD, you have it for life. Remember, however, that OCD is highly treatable with medication and behavior therapy. With proper care, you can minimize your symptoms and maximize your quality of life. In addition, tremendous breakthroughs have been made in the diagnosis and treatment of OCD over the course of the past ten years, and we continue to learn more about this disease every day.

Chapter 2
THE SYMPTOMS OF OCD

How can I evaluate the seriousness of my obsessions and compulsions?

Degree of seriousness is a function of the nature of your symptoms, your feelings about them, and your ability (or inability) to control them. If you have one or two symptoms and they do not interfere with your life, you're probably just fine. For example, many people find that keeping their desks neat—even what some might call "obsessively neat"—helps them to stay organized and meet deadlines. But if your day is squandered on arranging the papers on your desk just so and lining them up in a certain order again and again, leaving you little time to get anything else done, you should seek help.

Another important factor to consider is how you feel about the thoughts and rituals that consume the hours of your day. Guilt, shame, and anxiety are usual companions to OCD, whose sufferers take no pleasure in their exaggerated fears and repeated rituals. If you're functioning at an adequate level and feel like you have things under control, that's a good sign. On the other hand, if you are aware that your behavior is at times irrational and excessive but still find it virtually impossible to control, you may be suffering from obsessive-compulsive disorder and should see your doctor.

My sister thinks I may have a problem with OCD. Should I take this seriously?

Your family or the person you live with can some-times be more objective than you and may be very helpful in noting your problems. When others share their concerns about your behavior, it's prob-ably time for some good self-examination. If the thoughts and behavior you read about here de-scribe you, see your doctor.

When do close attention to detail and everyday "obsessiveness" become OCD?

Everyone has doubts and worries, but obsessions and compulsions are a far cry from normal or even excessive concerns about real-life problems. Ordi-nary thoughts and habits evolve into obsessions and compulsive rituals only when they become ir-rational and begin to intrude significantly upon day-to-day life. For example, many of us can relate to habits such as making sure the doors and win-dows are locked before going to bed at night. Checking and even double-checking to make sure your home is secure is a wise and reasonable thing to do—but rechecking fifty to one hundred times is excessive and unrealistic and robs you of valuable sleep. You may have crossed the line from obsessive tendencies to OCD when repeated, unnecessary, and seemingly unstoppable thoughts or actions take up an hour or more of each day and cause you great distress.

Are obsessions always accompanied by compulsions?

No. Some people have what are known as pure obsessions. These are extremely upsetting and disturbing thoughts that have no corresponding rituals. Often these thoughts or images are of violent, blasphemous, or sexually inappropriate actions that you would never dream of taking.

What are the typical symptoms of OCD?

People with OCD display a very wide range of symptoms. In fact, symptoms can be so distinct from one another that it is sometimes hard to believe they are manifestations of the same disease. As you pass through the different stages of your life, you may experience a variety of obsessions and compulsions. Since OCD symptoms tend to overlap, you may also find that you experience more than one at a time. For example, a person who has a problem with contamination may also have fears of harming someone. In general, your symptoms will tend to fall within one or more of these typical categories:

Contamination Fears and Washing Rituals
The most common obsession by far is an unreasonable and exaggerated fear of contamination by dirt

and germs. Excessive hand-washing and bathing rituals are a frequent response, lasting as many as two, three, or four hours a day or even longer. These cleansings are different from normal washing, for even after scrubbing his hands until they are raw, an OCD sufferer may still not believe they are clean. Moreover, there is a ritualistic quality to the pattern of cleansing. Showers must be taken and hands washed in a very specific manner. There is usually a specific sequence, such as right hand first, beginning with the pinky and using twenty up-and-down strokes to thoroughly cleanse each additional finger before turning at last to the palm. If the order is disturbed in any way, the entire process must be repeated from the beginning. If the OCD sufferer believes in magical numbers, everything he does—including washing—must be done his magical number of times.

People who suffer from contamination fears have an enormous need to avoid all potential sources of infection and contagion, which to them include such innocuous objects as doorknobs, electric light switches, and newspapers. Not surprisingly, therefore, shaking hands with strangers and using public rest rooms are especially anxiety-filled events. Over the last two decades, despite their apparent lack of exposure, a dread of AIDS has stricken many people with contamination fears.

Paradoxically, many of those obsessed with cleanliness end up being quite unkempt. Consider the example of wealthy movie mogul Howard Hughes: When he found that he couldn't completely eliminate germs from his environment, he eventually threw up his hands in despair and lived in squalor. Toward the end he rarely washed, no longer cut his hair or fingernails, and hoarded his own urine in jars. Fortunately, with the effective treatments available today, this sort of tragedy need no longer occur.

Hoarding Rituals

It may be that you're sentimental and stow away some old clothes in a trunk up in the attic, perhaps including your daughter's christening dress or your own wedding gown. There's nothing whatsoever wrong with this. But hoarders are unable to distinguish between what is of value, sentimental or otherwise, and what is just plain junk. They are unable to throw away out-of-date newspapers, old notes, ticket stubs, or empty boxes and bottles. One of these items may prove necessary and important someday—but they can't figure out just which one, and so they keep everything.

Hoarders save and even collect objects that have no intrinsic value. Perhaps there is some merit in saving playbills of shows you have seen, for example, to remember pleasant occasions in your life. But if you pick up playbills on the street of plays you have not seen and have no interest in, then you may have a problem.

Obsessions and Checking Rituals

"Checkers" can be driven by a variety of obsessive thoughts. Some are racked with doubt. Others constantly ask "Did I get it right? Did I do it or say it the right way?" Many experience guilt and an almost pathological fear that they have committed a serious error or oversight that will cause themselves or another grievous harm. For example, you may harbor an unreasonable belief that you have a terrible illness, and repeatedly call your physician or visit doctor after doctor in a vain attempt to verify your suspicions. Hypochondriacal concerns are very common in OCD, and even the continual reassurances of health care providers are usually to no avail.

When you are prone to checking rituals, it is often difficult to arrive anywhere on time or get anything accomplished. A checker may waste hours driving over the same section of a road again and again to make sure that he has not hit a pedestrian or caused an accident. Some checkers even get out of the car to look for evidence, such as tire tracks and oil spills, while others call the police station to see if an accident has been reported. They have trouble trusting what they see with their own eyes.

Checkers often have an excessive need for symmetry and order. Until the closet or desk is arranged in a certain way, they cannot make a move. Others have a drive to do everything perfectly. To many checkers, it seems almost impossible to pay the bills and balance the checkbook each month, since they have a compulsion to add up the same columns of figures again and again and again. They have an overwhelming need to "get it right." Leaving the house can also prove difficult, as there is that niggling doubt in the back of the mind: Did I lock the door? Close the windows? Feed the cat? Turn the iron off? Leave the gas on?

In spite of all evidence to the contrary, checkers are convinced that something is wrong, and they feel driven to repeatedly make sure they have done everything possible to ensure the safety of themselves and others. Thus they become locked into relentlessly rigid, unforgiving, and inordinately time-consuming rituals. In her anxiety and fear about causing a fire and burning the house down, for example, an OCD sufferer may turn the car around again and again (if indeed she makes it as far as the car) and drive home to make sure that all the appliances are turned off. In severe cases this can easily happen dozens of times and for hours on end. Even when the appliances are unplugged, the OCD sufferer may remain uneasy, feeling that something important has been left undone. Like the checker who is afraid he caused an accident, she finds it difficult to trust in the reality of her own observations and perceptions.

Undoing Rituals

Sometimes checking alone is not enough, and OCD sufferers develop undoing rituals, such as repeating certain phrases or counting backward from one thousand to ward off disaster. They need to make doubly (and triply and quadruply) sure that all the i's are dotted and t's are crossed.

Undoing rituals are usually very rigidly defined.

They might include repeating actions or reciting a special phrase or prayer a certain number of times. Or they may have magical numbers—specific lucky or unlucky numbers to be, respectively, sought after and adhered to or assiduously avoided.

Superstitious Thoughts and Rituals

Although anyone can harbor a superstition such as knocking on wood for luck or fearing Friday the thirteenth, most of us don't allow superstitions to control our lives. In the context of obsessions and compulsions, however, superstitions such as "Step on a crack and break your mother's back" take on a whole new meaning. They are carried to pointless and unrealistic extremes.

To some OCD sufferers, superstitions grow larger than life. Just recall the scene in *As Good As It Gets* when Jack Nicholson's character bobs and weaves through pedestrian traffic on the sidewalk to avoid stepping on any cracks. And then there is the OCD sufferer who fears the number thirteen and therefore stays home from work on the thirteenth of each month, becomes immobilized with fear at thirteen minutes past each hour on the clock, and refuses to buy any item with a price tag that ends in thirteen cents or costs thirteen dollars.

Pure Obsessions

Pure obsessions are disturbing thoughts that do not have any corresponding rituals. These thoughts are often peculiarly upsetting, unnerving, and even reprehensible. The images involved may be distressingly graphic or pornographic. Sometimes the impulses are of a violent and aggressive nature that you would never dream of acting on, such as molesting a child or harming a loved one. Religious individuals may have uncontrollable blasphemous thoughts, such as desecrating an altar, shouting an obscenity in church, or urinating on a crucifix.

Even though they may be wildly inappropriate, detested, and unwanted, the OCD sufferer cannot get these thoughts and images out of his head. At some point, no longer able to bear them, an OCD sufferer with pure obsessions may eventually revert to undoing rituals—counting backward a certain number of times, reciting a prayer, or silently repeating a magical number or phrase—in order to dispel or suppress these awful thoughts and images.

Obsessional Slowness

Unlike most other OCD sufferers, people who have obsessional slowness do not try to control their symptoms. Instead of resisting them, they appear to be utterly absorbed in completing in exact order every aspect of their time-consuming rituals. Every little thing must be just right, just so, and in its proper place.

Simple tasks such as bathing and getting dressed can take hours for those who have obsessional slowness, as they are driven to adhere to very formal and rigid patterns. For example, a person might tap the shower stall three times, turn around twice, then enter and turn on the water with her left hand. If by some chance she tapped the stall only twice or turned on the water with her right hand, the entire sequence would have to be repeated from the very beginning.

Not surprisingly, obsessional slowness can significantly interfere with one's ability to function socially or professionally. An enormous preoccupation with order, symmetry, and perfection paradoxically leads to inefficiency if not chaos. Although the pure version of this kind of OCD is relatively rare, obsessional slowness plays a role in many other categories, such as washing, checking, arranging, ordering, and undoing.

What are some typical compulsions or rituals of OCD?

As you know by now, OCD sufferers carry out a number of different rituals in order to gain temporary relief from the distress and discomfort caused by obsessions. Unlike addictive behavior, such as drinking alcohol or overeating, from which people at least initially derive some pleasure, the compulsions that distinguish obsessive-compulsive disorder bring only shame and embarrassment. Following is a list of some of the most common rituals:

- Cleaning, as in washing hands or showering all day to get rid of perceived germs

- Checking, as in repeatedly questioning whether you remembered to lock the door, turn off the stove, or unplug the iron
- Counting, as in counting the same complicated string of numbers again and again
- Repeating, as in repeating a name or phrase to dispel anxiety
- Completing, as in performing a complicated series of steps in an exact order again and again, until they are done perfectly
- Hoarding, as in collecting and repeatedly counting and stacking useless items

Are some rituals more common than others?

Absolutely. Cleaning is by far the most common compulsion, followed by checking.

Does ritualistic behavior lessen the anxiety brought on by obsessions?

Rituals provide only very momentary and fleeting relief. Although it is meant to reduce distress or prevent some feared event, compulsive behavior does not succeed in this in any realistic way. For example, excessive hand-washing is not in truth the way to prevent cancer, nor will counting backward and forward a specified number of times for each "bad" thought prevent you from following through on a repugnant and bizarre impulse, such as harming a loved one or shooting a stranger.

In the long run giving in to the urge to perform

rituals just magnifies and prolongs the troublesome obsession-compulsion relationship that treatment with medication and therapy is meant to break. A good parallel example is the crack addict. If he has one more smoke, his immediate craving is gone— but the craving will soon come raging back, more powerful and demanding than ever.

Do obsessions and compulsions always accompany one another?

Not always. OCD may involve either obsessions or compulsions, although usually both are present, according to the *Diagnostic and Statistical Manual of Mental Disorders,* fourth edition, or *DSM-IV* (American Psychiatric Association, 1994), the "bible" of mental illness. At times obsessive thoughts alone may crowd the mind and disrupt one's ability to function adequately. Even when they are not followed by rituals, these thoughts can be profoundly disturbing, uncomfortable, and upsetting. And while most times repetitive behavior (such as praying, counting, or repeating) is meant to neutralize the dread of an obsession, this is not invariably the case.

Can OCD lead to other emotional problems?

Yes. When you squander long hours each day washing, checking, ordering, or obsessing, it's easy to become depressed, anxious, and demoralized. Emotional problems—especially depression—are believed to be brought on by the frustration of dealing with an obsessive-compulsive problem. In addition, more than a third of those who suffer from OCD have phobias, while others are afflicted with panic or eating disorders. Some OCD sufferers turn to alcohol or drugs in a misguided attempt to control uncomfortable symptoms. Coexisting problems such as these can make OCD more difficult both to diagnose and to treat.

What is the difference between OCD and generalized anxiety disorder?

The boundaries between obsessive-compulsive disorder and generalized anxiety disorder (GAD) are not always very distinct. GAD is characterized by excessive worry and apprehension that lasts for six months and interferes with normal functioning. It's been suggested that the concerns typical of generalized anxiety disorders may be more realistic than those of OCD. The *DSM-IV* offers as an example that a person with GAD might worry about losing a job, while someone with OCD might obsess about "the intrusive distressing idea that 'God' is 'dog' spelled backward." Yet whatever the murky distinctions between these two disorders finally turn out to be, one thing that is clear is that the anxiety of OCD is no less intense and distressing and fully real to its sufferers than that of generalized anxiety disorders.

What are the symptoms of depression?

Depression is more than just feeling down in the dumps. This mood disorder is potentially a very serious illness that strikes one in every ten Americans, and two-thirds of those with OCD. The most common complication of OCD, depression is an isolating illness that can affect your relationships with family and friends and disrupt your work.

The symptoms of depression include sleep and appetite changes, sadness, guilt, shame, low self-esteem, anxiety, and extreme fatigue that last for over two weeks. If you experience these symptoms, you should see a mental health professional for evaluation and therapy. Make an appointment at once if you have any thoughts of harming yourself. Read more about this condition in *If You Think You Have Depression* by Roger Granet, M.D., and Robin K. Levinson.

What are phobias?

Phobias are irrational, intense, and often disabling fears of objects or situations, when there is no real danger. A specific phobia is a fear of a particular object or situation. People who have specific phobias can become abnormally terrified of small spaces such as elevators (claustrophobia), leaving the house or other familiar territory (agoraphobia), or flying (aerophobia). Social phobia is a more generalized fear of being painfully embarrassed in social situations.

It's easy to see how phobias can dovetail with OCD. For example, Frederick the Great, the eighteenth-century king of Prussia, was terrified of water and had his servants clean his body with dry towels. It's more than likely that he suffered from contamination fears in addition to a phobic fear of water.

What are panic attacks?

These are repeated episodes of sudden, unprovoked, and intense anxiety, fear, and discomfort. Physical symptoms include a rapid heartbeat, dizziness, nausea, shortness of breath, and a general feeling of loss of control. For a more extensive discussion of panic attacks, you can read *If You Think You Have Panic Disorder* by Roger Granet, M.D., and Robert Aquinas McNally. Since panic attacks and heart attacks have similar symptoms and can be mistaken for one another, prompt medical attention is necessary.

Do "compulsive" eaters, sex addicts, and substance abusers have OCD?

Probably not. Although people who overeat, act promiscuously, or abuse alcohol or drugs have problems they feel they can't stop, at least initially they derive some pleasure from these activities. In contrast, OCD sufferers take no pleasure in their obsessions and compulsions.

Are other forms of behavior disorders related to OCD?

Yes. In fact, up to ten percent of the American population is estimated to suffer from spectrum disorders genetically related to OCD. These include Tourette's syndrome, trichotillomania, body dysmorphic disorder, and autism.

There's a lot of debate in the scientific community about just how these and other disorders—for example, gambling addictions and hypochondriasis—relate to OCD. But whatever the exact biological connections are eventually revealed to be, it's useful to examine the similarities in these diseases in order to find more effective treatments for them.

What is Tourette's syndrome?

Tourette's is a severe type of tic disorder that first appears before the age of eighteen. A tic is a sudden, rapid, repeated movement or vocalization. Tics, unlike compulsions, are completely involuntary. They are not deliberate attempts to neutralize the anxiety of obsessions, nor do they adhere to the very formal, rigid, and ritualistic patterns of compulsions.

The vocal tics of Tourette's might include sounds such as snorting, sniffing, mumbling, stuttering, grunting, barking, or coughing. About one in ten people who suffer from Tourette's also uncontrollably spout obscenities. Motor tics include touching, squatting, deep knee bends, hopping, skipping, and twirling or retracing steps while walking. It's very common for someone who has Tourette's to also experience obsessions and compulsions.

What is trichotillomania?

Trichotillomania is the urge to compulsively pull out your own hair, typically one strand at a time. Unlike OCD, which is equally common in men and women, trichotillomania is almost exclusively a women's disease. Bald spots or complete baldness can be the result of constant tugging on scalp hair, and many women who have this disease must wear wigs. Eyelashes, eyebrows, and pubic hair may also be pulled. Women who suffer from trichotillomania say that it feels good to pull their hair out because it relieves stress and pressure.

What is body dysmorphic disorder?

Body dysmorphic disorder, or BDD, is a crippling preoccupation with an imagined defect or minor imperfection in one's appearance. Often people with BDD are preoccupied with the size and shape of their noses or with their complexions. They may repeatedly check perceived defects in the mirror and avoid socializing with others because they are painfully embarrassed about their appearance. Yet it is more than likely that no one else gives a second thought to either their profile or their facial imperfections.

What is autism?

Autism is a developmental disability that interferes with reasoning, social interaction, and communication skills. Common problems associated with autism include obsessive-compulsive behavior, aggression, anxiety, and hyperactivity. Repetitive body movements, checking, ordering, collecting, and arranging are all typical of autism. When there is a significant amount of obsessive-compulsive behavior, there may also be a good deal of aggressiveness.

If I have other emotional problems in addition to OCD, do they require treatment too?

In most cases, yes. When depression or other problems accompany an obsessive-compulsive disorder, you must deal with them as well as with your OCD. Perhaps you're keyed up with anxieties and fears, or conversely so tired and exhausted that you feel that you can't go on. Either way, without first straightening out these other problems, you won't be able to focus on the treatment—especially exposure-and-response prevention—that will help you control OCD. Your first step toward wellness is getting an accurate diagnosis of OCD and any other accompanying disorders.

Chapter 3

MAKING THE DIAGNOSIS

How is OCD diagnosed?

Obsessive-compulsive disorder is diagnosed by your physician or therapist after talking in depth with you about your symptoms. The diagnosis will be based on her own observations and also on the information you give her. If you are experiencing recurrent unwanted thoughts and/or ritualistic behavior that is disrupting your life, of which you are ashamed, and over which you have little or no control, it is likely that the diagnosis will be OCD.

What other tools might a therapist use to make the diagnosis?

A more scientific way to diagnose OCD is the use of a symptom checklist called the Yale-Brown Obsessive Compulsive Scale, or Y-BOCS. Developed by Dr. Wayne Goodman, Dr. Steven Rasmussen, and their associates, this exhaustive test can help identify your major symptoms and assess the severity of your disorder. Y-BOCS is an excellent diagnostic tool because it looks at all the different aspects of OCD. It can measure how much distress you experience, how it interferes with your ability to function socially and career-wise, and how much of your time is occupied by obsessive thoughts and compulsive behavior.

Are any medical tests used to diagnose obsessive-compulsive disorder?

While OCD is most likely caused by problems with the neurotransmitter serotonin in the brain, at this time there are no laboratory tests to determine whether you suffer from this problem.

What questions might the therapist ask me in order to determine whether I have OCD?

While some of us might answer yes to several of the following questions, many yes answers can indicate the presence of an obsessive-compulsive disorder:

- Do you shower and wash your hands much more frequently than do your friends or family members?
- Do you ever develop skin rashes from excessive washing?
- Are your bathroom routines very ritualized, and do they take hours?
- Do you worry about shaking hands with strangers or using public rest rooms?
- Do you keep your home so clean that you could eat off the kitchen floor?
- Are you unreasonably concerned about acquiring a serious disease such as AIDS or cancer?

- Do you continually seek reassurance from your friends that your nose is not too big or you don't have bad breath?

- Do you check things over and over again, even though you really know that the emergency brake is off and you already locked the door?

- Do you pat your pockets constantly to make sure that you have not lost your wallet or sunglasses?

- When you go into a restaurant you've visited on dozens of occasions, do you still ask them one more time if they accept credit cards?

- Are you very worried that you did something wrong that will cause your house to be robbed or flooded or burned down?

- Are you overly concerned about accidentally hitting someone with your car?

- Do you worry about harm befalling a family member or close friend because you weren't careful enough?

- Do you have disturbing thoughts that you cannot control no matter how hard you try?

- Do you have unwanted sickening sexual thoughts about strangers, animals, or children?

- Do you experience unwanted aggressive thoughts about harming a loved one?

- Do you have unwanted blasphemous thoughts?

- Are you overly concerned with keeping your clothing or shoes arranged in a very exact order?

- Do you feel compelled to straighten the pens on your desk or the books on your shelves?

- Are you upset when someone "messes up" the order of your clothing, shoes, pens, or books?

- Do you have a compulsion to save old newspapers, boxes, notes, cards, candy wrappers, or empty baby-food jars?

- Do you feel a need to count objects like the tiles on the floor, the books in a bookcase, the seeds in a watermelon, or even the grains of sand on the beach?

- Do you perform a mental ritual, such as repeating a phrase or saying a prayer, to "undo" any bad thoughts you might have?

- Are you superstitious? Do you avoid certain numbers (such as thirteen), step over cracks, or knock on wood?

- Do you have magical numbers?

- Do you feel compelled to perform activities a magical or lucky number of times?

- Do you follow an exact and complicated sequence of steps in order to get dressed or showered or enter your house? If you miss a step, do you keep starting over from the beginning again until you get it right?

- Do you have an obsessive need to memorize insignificant details such as license plate numbers, old telephone numbers, out-of-date subway lines, and obscure song lyrics?

What kind of psychiatric disorder is OCD?

OCD is an anxiety disorder. Anxiety disorders—which include generalized anxiety disorders, phobias, panic disorders, and post-traumatic stress syndrome as well as OCD—are exhausting illnesses in which you feel anxious and upset for no real reason. Although there is no true outside trigger of distress, this anxiety feels just as real as the anxiety you would experience if your plane were about to crash or if someone were breaking into your home. The same chemical reactions are taking place in your brain as when those real anxiety-producing events take place, and the OCD sufferer has no way of telling that these are really the equivalent of false alarms going off in the brain.

What impact can I expect anxiety to have on my life?

The anxiety generated by obsessions and compulsions can drain your energy and wreak havoc in your life. The American Psychiatric Association's *DSM-IV* puts it this way: "Because obsessive intrusions can be distracting, they frequently result in inefficient performance of cognitive tasks that require concentration, such as reading or computation. . . . Performing compulsions may become a major life activity, leading to serious marital, occupational, or social disability. Pervasive avoidance may leave an individual housebound."

How are anxiety disorders different from the normal anxieties of day-to-day life?

Everyone knows what normal anxiety feels like—the tension in your stomach before taking a test, tossing and turning all night when you have to make a speech the next morning, the butterflies in your stomach on a first date, or a pounding heart when you're trapped in traffic and trying to get to a job interview on time. A certain amount of anxiety is a good thing. It heightens your senses and makes you more alert. It rouses you to action, making your adrenaline flow so you will perform your best under pressure.

In contrast, anxiety disorders disrupt your life without making any such positive or useful contributions. While OCD anxiety has no tangible trigger—no test, no speech, no date, no interview—your body doesn't know that, and the distress feels just as real. This is because the same chemical reactions occur in the brain when there is a real threatening situation and when an OCD sufferer perceives a threat that doesn't really exist. False alarms go off in the brain—but the OCD sufferer has no way of knowing they are false alarms.

How is OCD different from other anxiety disorders?

In making a diagnosis of obsessive-compulsive disorder, your therapist will keep in mind what distinguishes OCD from other anxiety disorders:

- OCD affects men and women equally. Other anxiety disorders primarily affect women.
- OCD occurs at a younger age than panic disorders.
- OCD responds primarily to pharmaceutical treatment with SRIs (serotonin-reuptake inhibitors).

What is the difference between OCD and obsessive-compulsive personality disorder?

Although they have similar names, these are two different diseases. Obsessive-compulsive personality disorder "involves a pervasive pattern of preoccupation with orderliness, perfectionism, and control," according to *DSM-IV*. It is not characterized by obsessions and compulsions.

What is the difference between suffering from OCD and having an obsessive style?

Some of us are neatniks and can't relax until the house is spotless. Others of us worry, perhaps excessively, when our teenagers have the car. But everyday habits and worries like these do not mean that you have a disease. Ordinary doubts, thoughts, and habits are very different from the obsessions and rituals of OCD, which are irrational, profoundly upsetting, and intrude significantly on your day-to-day life.

I wash my hands again and again every day, but still they never seem clean. I'm anxious and unhappy. Am I suffering from OCD or depression?

Good question. You may have a psychiatric problem, but only your therapist can determine whether you are suffering from obsessive-compulsive disorder, depression, both, or neither condition.

Sometimes OCD and depression are so closely linked that it's difficult to distinguish between them. But while their symptoms often seem to grow better or worse at the same times, obsessive-compulsive disorder and depression are in reality two different illnesses.

In the past, the American Psychiatric Association excluded a diagnosis of OCD when depression was present. But now the *DSM-IV* says that you may be diagnosed with both OCD and depression, as long as the obsession is not too close in content to the source or preoccupations of your depression.

How is OCD different from hypochondriasis?

Hypochondriasis is actually similar to OCD in many ways. Like an OCD sufferer, a hypochondriac thinks he is ill when no real illness is present. The difference is that in hypochondriasis, fears alone are present. In a person with OCD, unsubstantiated concerns about having a serious disease such as cancer or AIDS are followed by rituals like excessive washing or checking. Underlining their similarities again, however, is the fact that hypochondriasis responds to the same medications as OCD.

How long does the average person wait between the onset of OCD and seeking professional help?

Unfortunately, people with obsessive-compulsive symptoms sometimes try to hide their condition due to shame or embarrassment and wait far too long before seeking treatment. In fact, one study found the average wait to be as long as ten years, followed by another seven years until appropriate treatment was given. In addition to reluctance on the part of OCD sufferers, this astonishing time lapse can be attributed to a general lack of knowledge about OCD. As we come to a greater understanding of this disease, the time period can be dramatically shortened.

Why does OCD diagnosis take so long?

There are a number of reasons. Other disorders, such as depression or anxiety, can cause some of the same symptoms as OCD, and overlapping symptoms such as tension and guilt can make diagnosis difficult. But perhaps even more significantly, people who have OCD have traditionally hidden their condition from the rest of the world. With growing knowledge that OCD is a largely biological illness that is nobody's fault, it is hoped that this attitude will dissipate and that sufferers will more promptly seek treatment.

Is everyone with OCD aware that they have a problem?

For the most part, yes. In fact, the American Psychiatric Association stresses that by definition individuals with OCD are aware that their obsessions are intrusive and inappropriate. People with OCD experience their thoughts as "ego-dystonic"; that is, they are uncomfortable with their alien thoughts, which are not at all the kind of thoughts they would want or expect to have, and yet they cannot control them.

There are two exceptions to this rule. Children are not generally aware that their obsessions and compulsions are excessive and unreasonable, nor are a small number of adults. Not mincing words, the *DSM-IV* specifies that these are adults "with poor insight."

Does OCD come on gradually or suddenly?

In most cases, OCD creeps up on you. The development of symptoms takes place gradually over time. Occasionally, however, there have been sudden onsets.

Do recurrent episodes of OCD vary in nature?

Yes. Both the variety and the intensity of OCD symptoms wax and wane over the years, and of course the symptoms also vary widely from person to person. Most OCD sufferers find that obsessions and compulsions worsen during stressful times, such as the loss of a loved one, a divorce, a move, or a job change; at other times they may scarcely know that they suffer from the disorder. For an unlucky few, however, symptoms are more or less constant and significantly interfere with their careers and private lives.

Symptoms themselves also change over time. As a child with OCD, you might have experienced washing symptoms, but as an adult, you may find yourself checking, counting, or experiencing uncomfortable obsessive thoughts.

Are some races or cultures more prone to OCD than others?

No. OCD is color- and culture-blind, affecting people at all economic levels in countries all around the world.

Does OCD run in families?

Yes, there is some evidence of this. Identical twins are more likely than fraternal twins to both have OCD. And if an immediate family member has OCD, you are more likely to develop this problem.

Are women more prone to OCD than men?

Absolutely not. In contrast to other anxiety disorders, which affect primarily women, OCD strikes men and women in equal numbers.

Are there any differences between OCD in men and OCD in women?

Obsessive-compulsive symptoms are basically the same in men and women, but a few minor differences occur in their timing. One variation lies in the average age of onset. Males usually develop obsessive-compulsive symptoms between the ages of 6 and 15, while in women the average age of occurrence is between 20 and 29. In addition, female hormones may play a role in the waxing and waning of symptoms in women.

At what age does OCD usually develop?

OCD usually begins in adolescence or early adulthood, but it may also occur in childhood. Onethird to one-half of adults report that they first experienced symptoms as children. OCD rarely occurs for the first time in senior citizens.

How common is OCD in children?

OCD may affect as many as one in two hundred children. These numbers may even understate the frequency of the problem, since many children (like adults) are embarrassed by their symptoms and try to hide them. Many school-age children also have an OCD-related tic disorder.

What are tics?

Tics are sudden and involuntary repeated movements or vocalizations. They include sounds such as snorting, sniffing, mumbling, stuttering, grunting, barking, or coughing. Common motor tics are touching, squatting, deep knee bends, hopping, skipping, and twirling or retracing steps while walking. A well-known tic disorder is Tourette's syndrome.

What is OCD in children like?

Children who have OCD can't sit still. They fuss and fidget. According to the American Psychiatric Association's *DSM-IV*, symptoms of OCD in children are roughly similar to those in adults. Washing, checking, and ordering are especially common rituals in this age group. Children with OCD may also exhibit the restlessness normally associated with attention deficit hyperactivity disorder (ADHD), and in fact many children who have OCD also suffer from ADHD. Other obsessive-compulsive symptoms in children include excessive hoarding and compulsive movements.

What is the difference between OCD in children and in adults?

A major diagnostic difference is that children are not necessarily aware that their obsessions or compulsions are excessive or unreasonable. And since they do not know that they have a problem, children don't tend to seek out any special help. A decline in the ability to do schoolwork due to poor concentration may tip parents off to a problem. Otherwise OCD in children is similar to OCD in adults.

I've heard that strep throat in children can lead to OCD and tic disorders. Is this true?

Growing evidence does indeed point to a link between group A beta-hemolytic streptococci and these disorders. In susceptible children a strep throat can trigger an autoimmune response affecting the basal ganglia and leading to the symptoms of obsessive-compulsive and tic disorders. PANDAS is the acronym that has been given to children who have "pediatric autoimmune neuropsychiatric disorders associated with streptococcal infections."

Is it my fault that my child suffers from OCD?

Most likely not. In the past, OCD was thought to be the result of unconscious conflicts over control issues during childhood. Over the past ten years or so, this was shown not to be the case. While it is true that OCD runs in families, there is nothing to suggest that it is due to poor parenting. Current research strongly suggests that OCD is a purely biological problem linked with changes in brain chemicals.

How can I help my child or other family member with OCD?

No matter what causes OCD, the good news is that it is possible to control this condition with a combination of medications and behavior therapy. There are many things you can do to help. First of all, don't give in to obsessions and rituals. The worst thing you can do is to go along with a family member's compulsive washing or checking rituals in order to avoid scenes and fights and to keep the peace. While giving in might make life easier in the short run, over time it only strengthens the link between obsessions and compulsions and makes matters worse.

It's also important for you to support the treatment regimen and make sure your child or other family member sticks to it. And if you try to keep in mind that OCD is an illness that is no one's fault, it may be easier for you to be more patient and control negative feelings such as anger and resentment. (Read more about what family members can do to help in Chapter 9.)

In addition to seeing a doctor or therapist, what else can I do to determine whether I have OCD?

In the United States each year, there is a free screening day for people who suspect they may suffer from an anxiety disorder such as OCD. National Anxiety-Disorder Screening Day (NADSD) takes place at designated sites in most large metropolitan areas around the country. A licensed mental health professional such as a psychologist or psychiatrist will be on hand to see you and help determine whether you have a psychiatric illness such as OCD. He or she will speak to you and probably ask you to fill out a questionnaire. If you need further evaluation or treatment, you will be referred to a local physician or mental health professional.

How can I find out when there will be a National Anxiety-Disorder Screening Day in my area?

The Obsessive-Compulsive Foundation (OCF) is a sponsor of National Anxiety-Disorder Screening Day. Contact them at (203) 878–5669 for further information.

Chapter 4
THE CAUSES OF OCD

What causes OCD?

The exact causes of OCD remain unknown. Research strongly suggests, however, that a biochemical imbalance is responsible. Scientists suspect that changes in the brain chemical systems that regulate repetitive behavior may eventually prove to be the root cause of OCD. Specifically, the neurotransmitter or brain chemical serotonin is thought to play a central role in obsessive-compulsive disorder. Since OCD tends to run in families, this tendency toward serotonin imbalance may be an inherited problem. Stress, although it does not directly cause OCD, may trigger and heighten its symptoms.

What role do neurotransmitters play in healthy brain function?

Your behavior, mood, and emotions are all dependent on efficient communication among the cells in your brain. Healthy brains in turn depend on normal interplay among chemicals called neurotransmitters. When there are problems with neurotransmitters such as serotonin, psychological and physiological symptoms can result.

How does communication in the brain normally work?

Your brain is the most important part of your nervous system. It is composed of nearly 100 billion neurons, or nerve cells, with many more neurons extending outward throughout the body. Information is transmitted through the nervous system via a network of electrical and chemical signals that travel from one neuron to the next.

Serotonin and other neurotransmitters travel from nerve cell to nerve cell across fluid-filled gaps called synapses, passing along messages about moods and emotions by attaching themselves to receptors on neighboring nerve cells. Messages can be happy or filled with trepidation. For example, if an outside stimulus causes you to be fearful, your brain would signal a fight-or-flight response, in which your heart would beat faster and your brain would go into high gear to help extract you from your difficulties. Special receptor chemicals on the next neuron in the chain of communication are prepared to receive this message from a neurotransmitter, and that neuron will pass it to the next one, and so on.

What happens when there is a problem with serotonin?

A slight abnormality in the neurotransmitter serotonin can throw off this entire sequence of communication in the brain. A communications failure occurs when serotonin is reabsorbed or sucked back into nerve cells instead of crossing the synapse. As vital chemical messages are lost, OCD symptoms develop, leading to the repetitive compulsions and rituals of OCD. Abnormalities in serotonin and other neurotransmitters (dopamine, norepinephrine, and the like) can also lead to other psychological problems such as depression.

Are there any theories as to what causes neurotransmitter abnormalities?

OCD seems to run in families. If your mother or brother has OCD, you too may have a potential problem with serotonin levels in your brain. This problem can lie dormant for years, until OCD symptoms are triggered—usually in late adolescence or early adulthood—by a series of stressful events. Stress lies in the eye of the beholder, and events affect each individual differently. But when you possess a genetic weakness, anything from taking your SATs to going away to college, to the death of a loved one, a job loss, or a move, can trigger the development or recurrence of OCD.

By the same token, a genetic predisposition for a disease does not necessarily mean that you will get it. The same holds true for cancer or heart disease. If a close family member has suffered from a problem such as OCD, breast cancer, or cardiovascular disease, you too are more likely to develop that problem—but it does not mean that you will. While you can't control whether you get a disease, you can control lifestyle factors such as stress, exercise, and diet, which act as contributing factors to many health problems.

What parts of the brain appear to be involved in OCD?

Tests of people with active OCD symptoms (for example, when someone who has contamination fears is asked to hold a dirty towel) show heightened activity in the brain area known as the orbital cortex, which is located just above your eyes behind your forehead. Three other areas deep inside the brain—the caudate nucleus, the cingulate gyrus, and the thalamus—also appear to be implicated in OCD. Scientists are continuing to use brain-imaging tests to learn more about what causes OCD and how to treat it.

What tests do scientists use to study OCD?

Technological advances including new brain-imaging methods and laboratory techniques are bringing scientists closer and closer to discovering the root causes of OCD. In recent years researchers have used imaging methods known as magnetic resonance imaging (MRI) and positron-emission tomography (PET scans) to observe how the brain functions in people who have OCD. These are research tools that you should not expect as part of your regular treatment for OCD.

What happens in an MRI?

MRIs—or magnetic resonance imaging—are often used to study the brains of people who have OCD. They are the safest and most sensitive imaging techniques available today. An MRI is usually a noninvasive procedure, although on occasion injections of dye are used. During an MRI procedure the patient is surrounded by a powerful magnetic field while radio waves pass through his head. The only potential discomfort experienced is mild claustrophobia, since the test takes place with the patient lying down in a hollow tube for thirty to sixty minutes. Visualization or meditation, or even a mild tranquilizer, can be used to counter discomfort. MRIs cannot be performed on people who have pacemakers.

What happens in a PET scan?

PET scans show what parts of the brain are active. In a PET scan radioactively labeled glucose is injected into the patient. The glucose solution, which emits very active particles called positrons, is absorbed by brain cells. Positron-emission tomography, similar to X-rays, is then used to measure which parts of the brain are taking up the most glucose. These parts—metabolically the most active—appear to be the areas involved with OCD.

Has brain-imaging technology led to any new theories about OCD?

Yes. Dr. Jeffrey Schwartz, an expert in OCD and the author of *Brain Lock,* believes that the tight and hyperactive linkage among these four parts of the brain—the orbital cortex, the caudate nucleus, the cingulate gyrus, and the thalamus—cause a situation called "brain lock," leading to repetitive and intrusive thoughts and habits. Dr. Schwartz considers OCD to be a "shake in the mind," similar to the tremors of Parkinson's disease. Both disorders are characterized by disturbances in the basal ganglia; Parkinson's causes abnormal movements, while OCD leads to abnormal thoughts.

What happens in "brain lock"?

Brain lock begins when the orbital cortex alerts the brain to a potential problem. For example, if a stranger is following you home at night, or even when you're late for an appointment and stuck in traffic, alarms kick in. These are valid and normal concerns that would normally raise anyone's anxiety level. In people who have OCD, however, the orbital cortex becomes hyperactive and sends out the equivalent of a false alarm.

When a false signal reaches other parts of the brain—notably the caudate nucleus (a part of the basal ganglia that helps in switching gears from one thought to another), the cingulate gyrus (which makes your stomach churn and your heart beat faster), and the thalamus (which processes signals from the cortex and other areas)—anxiety results. Since there is no real cause for distress, your brain ordinarily turns off the panic button; common sense prevails, and your thought processes return to normal. But in the overcharged brains of those who have OCD, this doesn't happen. Instead, all four brain areas lock into a hyperactive overdrive, frantically zinging inaccurate distress signals back and forth to one another. According to the "brain lock" theory, this results in the obsessions and compulsions of OCD.

Is there any way to cure "brain lock"?

Research published by Dr. Schwartz and his colleagues at UCLA indicates that successful behavior therapy can produce the same cerebral changes as successful drug therapy. When the brain is unstuck or unlocked, OCD symptoms recede. Therapy involves relabeling obsessive thoughts as disease symptoms and refocusing attention on a positive activity (instead of an anxiety-reducing ritual), such as a hobby. The idea is that the more you ignore intrusive thoughts, the less you are bothered by oppressive obsessions.

Does behavior therapy always reduce "brain lock"?

No therapy thus far has shown 100 percent success in controlling the symptoms of OCD. Neither drugs nor therapy—nor even the two in combination—always works. But after ten weeks of behavior therapy alone (with no medication), twelve out of eighteen patients at UCLA showed reduced metabolic activity in PET scans and a corresponding drop in the severity of OCD symptoms.

Are there other theories about the biological causes of OCD?

Yes. Recent research has opened up new paths of inquiry into the role of infection in OCD. A team led by scientist Dr. Susan Swedo at the National Institute of Mental Health (NIMH) has uncovered an intriguing link between childhood strep throat and OCD.

What is the link between childhood strep throat and obsessive-compulsive symptoms?

Dr. Swedo and her team have discovered a relationship between group A beta-hemolytic streptococci and obsessive-compulsive symptoms and tic disorders. In susceptible children antibodies attack the basal ganglia in the brain, which leads to fears of contamination and obsessive-compulsive behavior such as excessive washing, hoarding, checking, arranging, symmetry rituals, and compulsive movements. Dr. Swedo has dubbed this phenomenon PANDAS, an acronym for children who have "pediatric autoimmune neuropsychiatric disorders associated with streptococcal infections."

Does strep cause permanent OCD?

Most obsessive-compulsive symptoms caused by strep clear up over time, but repeated infections—

some so mild that they may not even be noticed—
can lead to OCD and verbal tics.

What makes a child susceptible to this problem?

No one knows for sure, but a number of different
factors may be involved. Having a parent with
OCD appears to increase the risk, or there may
have been a trauma to the basal ganglia during
childbirth, rendering a child more susceptible to
further injury later on. Immunological factors or
mutant strains of strep bacteria may also be responsible.

Is there anything I can do to protect my child?

When a child experiences a sudden onset of obsessive-compulsive symptoms or tics, Dr. Swedo rec-
ommends a throat culture for both the child and
her family. Prompt intervention with penicillin and
gamma globulin can relieve behavioral symptoms.

Are there also environmental causes of OCD?

Unlike most other psychiatric disorders, scientists
believe that OCD is probably caused by biochemical imbalances alone. This new theory of OCD
stands in stark contrast to beliefs closely held
until only ten or twenty years ago. Until recent
times OCD was attributed to problems such as
control issues or coming from a dysfunctional
family.

If environmental factors do not cause OCD, do they contribute to it in any way?

While environmental factors do not *cause* OCD, they definitely contribute to it. Stress and emotional trauma can trigger or worsen the symptoms of OCD.

Does this mean that anyone under stress can develop obsessions and compulsions?

No. The most likely underlying cause of OCD is a genetic predisposition to the disease. Stress is an environmental trigger of OCD, meaning that it does not directly cause obsessions and compulsions but may trigger or aggravate their development or recurrence in susceptible individuals.

What causes stress?

Stress is closely associated with the challenges in our lives and our abilities to cope with them. If the challenges are too great, beyond our resources to handle them, we experience stress. Likewise, if our abilities and resources are much greater than our challenges, we also experience stress. The goal is to reach a balance of challenge and ability.

How does stress trigger obsessive-compulsive symptoms?

The loss of a close friend or family member, a move, a job loss, or financial problems put you under an enormous amount of pressure and strain.

When you experience this kind of emotional trauma, your body responds by secreting extra amounts of hormones from the adrenal glands. Increased levels of hormones for extended periods of time can produce changes in the brain, possibly resulting in changes in behavior. Cumulative stress in your life makes you vulnerable to diseases to which you have a hereditary vulnerability.

What is the fight-or-flight response?

Our bodies respond to stress with a surge of hormones that prepare us for "fight or flight." Long ago this response served a very practical purpose: It got our adrenaline going so we could fight our enemies or, alternatively, run away from them. Today we live in an asphalt jungle where the enemies we confront are likely to be irate bosses and rude taxi drivers. Although our bodies still respond with the same hormonal surges, fight and flight are no longer appropriate responses. What is left are the physical reactions of increased heart rate and breathing, elevated blood pressure, and decreased digestive function. This makes us more susceptible to any number of health problems.

This sounds like how I feel when I experience anxious thoughts and urges to ritualize. Is it the same thing?

Basically, yes. Sometimes the overwhelming anxiety felt by OCD sufferers is triggered by stress; at other times there is no outside cause at all. It is a matter of neurons misfiring in your brain and causing the equivalent of a false alarm. Nonetheless, the resulting anxiety is painfully real.

Is stress always a bad thing?

A certain amount of eu-stress (the good kind) can motivate you to do your best on an exam or meet an important deadline at the office. But when most of us think about stress, it is in terms of challenges and experiences that are beyond our ability to control. This kind of stress is bad for your health.

What are the most stress-inducing life events?

One way to measure stress is by ranking the anxiety level generated by different life events. Starting from the most stressful, these events include:

- Death of a spouse
- Divorce
- Marital separation
- Jail term
- Death of a close family member
- Personal injury or illness
- Marriage
- Getting fired from a job
- Marital problems
- Retirement

- A health change in a family member
- Pregnancy
- Sexual problems
- New family member
- Business readjustment
- Change in finances
- Death of a close friend
- Career change
- Change in number of arguments with your spouse
- Home mortgage or other major loan
- Foreclosure on a mortgage or loan
- Change in responsibilities at work
- Son or daughter leaving home
- Trouble with in-laws
- Outstanding personal achievement
- Spouse begins or stops work
- Beginning or finishing school
- Change in living conditions
- Revision of personal habits
- Trouble with employer
- Change in working hours or conditions
- Change in residence
- Change in school
- Change in recreation
- Change in church activities
- Change in social activities

- Minor loan
- Change in sleeping habits
- Vacation
- Christmas
- Minor violations of the law

What, if anything, do all these events have in common?

The most damaging kinds of stressful situations are those that we cannot control. Change that is beyond our ability to control is a common denominator in all these stress-inducing events. Stress relates to our ability to cope with changes and challenges in our lives.

Is there a connection between depression and OCD?

Yes. These two diseases often occur together—but depression does not cause stress. In fact, it's the other way around. Depression is believed to be brought on by the frustration of coping with obsessions and compulsions. It occurs in about half of people who have OCD.

People tell me I should "just get over it." They say I should stop this nonsense and move on with my life. Are they right?

Many people mistakenly believe that OCD is due to a simple lack of willpower. Unaware that it is a biologically driven disease, friends, family, and coworkers may attribute your unusual preoccupations and behavior to deficiencies in your character. They may think you're weak or lazy. Of course, nothing could be farther from the truth. OCD is an illness. Comments like these are made out of fear and ignorance.

How old is the average person with OCD?

Intrusive thoughts and repetitive rituals usually begin in adolescence or early adulthood. But one-third to one-half of adults initially experience symptoms as children.

If my mother or father has OCD, am I more likely to develop it?

Yes. OCD tends to run in families. For example, studies have shown that identical twins are more likely to have OCD than are fraternal twins. If an immediate family member has OCD, you are more likely to develop OCD symptoms.

Will scientists ever determine the exact cause of OCD?

While there is still no full explanation for OCD and much is left to discover, in recent years enormous strides have been made in determining its causes. In the past OCD was linked to unconscious conflicts, control issues, anger and guilt. Today scientists are exploring the roles of genes, brain chemicals, environmental triggers, and infection in obsessive-compulsive disorder. As we home in on the exact causes of OCD, there is increasing hope of finding help for early intervention and even more effective treatments.

Chapter 5
FINDING HELP

How can I tell if my problem is severe enough to warrant professional help?

On the surface, many obsessive concerns and repetitive rituals seem completely normal. For instance, many of us are concerned about safety and security, so we check to make sure the lights are off and the door is locked when we leave the office at the end of the day. And if every day your coworker buys a lottery ticket against all odds, using magical numbers from birthdays and addresses, who's to say he's abnormal?

Let's review what makes OCD different. People who have OCD take essentially harmless notions like these and carry them to unreasonable extremes, checking and rechecking again and again that the office door is locked and reciting magical numbers incessantly to ward off harm to loved ones and prevent other unimaginable disasters. As we saw earlier in this book, when your thoughts grow increasingly intrusive and rituals come to consume more and more of your time and energy, it is time to take stock of your situation. Remember to ask yourself these three questions:

- Is my behavior consuming an hour or more of my day?
- Are thoughts and rituals causing me severe distress, anxiety, guilt, or shame?
- Are they beginning to significantly interfere with my day-to-day life?

If your answers to these questions are yes, you may be suffering from OCD and should consult your doctor or a mental health professional.

Will OCD go away on its own if I don't seek treatment?

Probably not. The symptoms of OCD wax and wane, so mildly obsessive notions and rituals may be associated with stress that you are currently experiencing. Perhaps they will disappear when you make the adjustment to the current tense situation. But more likely, without the aid of medication or behavior therapy, to avoid anxiety you will give in to distressing urges by performing rituals such as cleaning and checking. Each time you do so, you deepen the hold your disease has on you.

Can my family doctor help me?

It's possible. Your regular family doctor is most likely an internist or family practitioner who had training in psychiatry in medical school. If she is someone you like and trust, you may feel comfortable discussing your problems with her. Possibly she can help you, or at least refer you on to a mental health specialist. Yet even though primary care physicians are the health care professionals most likely to encounter your obsessive-compulsive symptoms for the first time, they are often unable to make a proper diagnosis. There are several reasons for this.

What is it that prevents my regular doctor from diagnosing my problem?

Unfortunately, many family doctors have little hands-on experience with OCD. Although all doctors receive training in psychiatry, many may be unfamiliar with obsessive-compulsive disorders. This is particularly true of a doctor who was trained prior to the last ten years or so, during which a new understanding of OCD has emerged.

Another impediment to diagnosis is the current complicated and impersonal system of managed care. If you're like many consumers today, you may no longer even have a regular family doctor. If you belong to an HMO (health maintenance organization), your doctor may be whoever happens to be on duty when you visit your health care facility. Or you may see a nurse practitioner or doctor's assistant. Sadly, primary care providers no longer have much time or incentive to sit down and spend time with patients.

Finally, the greatest obstacle is that people with OCD are slow to seek medical treatment because their obsessions and compulsions frighten and embarrass them. They may feel confused about their disease and reluctant to be fully open about its symptoms. OCD sufferers know that something is wrong, but perhaps they haven't heard of OCD, so they have no idea that their symptoms have a name, an explanation, and a treatment. Clearly this is a significant hindrance to diagnosis.

Why are people who have OCD so reluctant to seek professional help?

Most people with OCD experience intense shame and embarrassment due to their illness. When you have OCD, you experience troubling thoughts that are persistent and unwanted. You are painfully aware that your behavior is peculiar and different from that of other people, and yet you cannot control it. You may experience a painful and almost overwhelming sense of anxiety and a fear that if others knew what you were thinking and doing, they'd believe you were crazy. So sadly, you suffer in silence.

It's especially horrifying to OCD sufferers when their obsessions center on lewd sexual images or thoughts of violence. Some can't stand to be around knives and other sharp objects for fear they will use them to harm someone. In fact, your memory can play tricks on you when you have OCD, and you may feel a need to be reassured that you did not already cut someone with that knife.

These intense feelings of shame and humiliation

often prevent people who have OCD from seeking medical treatment. But when they finally do see a therapist and learn that their irrational thoughts and rituals are caused by their illness, most are profoundly relieved. A huge weight is lifted off your shoulders when you realize that you're not going to do this terrible thing you're thinking about; you're just afraid that you will. A therapist can help you make this crucial distinction.

What is a mental health specialist?

A mental health specialist is a licensed professional trained in mental health, human behavior, and interpersonal relationships, who can diagnose and treat psychiatric illnesses and emotional disorders. Mental health professionals—commonly referred to as therapists—include psychiatrists, psychologists, clinical social workers, and psychiatric nurses.

- Psychiatrists are medical doctors who have completed special training and residency in psychiatry.

- Psychologists have completed a doctoral degree in psychology.

- Clinical social workers have a master's degree in social work and are trained in counseling.

- Psychiatric nurses have a master's degree in psychiatric nursing.

What do the different types of mental health specialists have in common?

All these specialists may help people with mental disorders such as OCD. In all these categories it's important to seek out therapists who have specific experience with anxiety disorders and behavior therapy.

How do I know which type of practitioner to see?

Once you have received a positive diagnosis of OCD, you are on the right track. If a therapist rather than a primary care provider diagnosed your problem, consider starting therapy with her. If an internist made the call, ask for a recommendation to a therapist with a specific background in OCD. Many mental health specialists are now familiar with selective serotonin-reuptake inhibitors such as Prozac, and it is easy to find a psychiatrist who can prescribe drugs. But it is more difficult to locate a psychiatrist or other therapist who is experienced in treating OCD sufferers with exposure-and-response prevention.

What kind of training do psychiatrists get?

Psychiatrists are medical doctors who specialize in the diagnosis and treatment of mental or psychiatric disorders. Their training consists of medical school, internship, and a three-year residency in the diagnosis and treatment of psychiatric disorders.

Psychiatrists can prescribe medication and admit you to a hospital if necessary.

Do all psychiatrists routinely prescribe medication for OCD patients?

No. These decisions are made on a case-by-case basis. Your psychiatrist will meet with you to evaluate your symptoms and devise an individualized treatment plan based on your needs. If your anxiety is intense and if thoughts and rituals are significantly interfering with your day-to-day life, you may need medication to jump-start your behavior therapy. If you are too anxious or depressed, you will otherwise be unable to focus on exposure-and-response prevention.

What kind of training do psychologists receive?

Psychologists complete a graduate program in human psychology that includes clinical training and internship in counseling, psychotherapy, and psychological testing. Psychologists are not medical doctors, but they do have doctoral degrees. They may have a Ph.D. or Psy.D. in clinical psychology, or a Ph.D. or Ed.D. in counseling psychology. They cannot prescribe drugs. Most states require some kind of licensing procedure before a psychologist can practice independently.

What is the difference between psychiatrists and psychologists?

The main difference is that psychiatrists have attended medical school and can prescribe medications. Psychiatrists have an M.D. after their name.

What is a clinical social worker?

Licensed clinical social workers (L.C.S.W.s) are therapists who complete a two-year graduate program with specialized training in helping people with mental health problems. Most states require some kind of exam and licensing procedure.

What is a psychiatric nurse?

Psychiatric nurses are health care professionals who have special training and experience in coping with mental illness as well as a master's degree in nursing. There are no special licensing or certification requirements for psychiatric nurses to act as therapists.

Are mental health services generally covered by health insurance?

Coverage depends on your diagnosis and the type of insurance you have. Health plans generally distinguish between physical illness and mental illness, ignoring the fact that many mental illnesses—including OCD—have biochemical causes. Health plans usually limit the number of mental health visits you are entitled to in a year. In most cases there are also larger copayments and a lifetime cap on how much they will pay for mental health visits.

What should I do if my insurance doesn't cover the cost of my care?

Ask your therapist whether she offers a sliding scale (a discount for those who cannot pay the full fee). Alternatively, contact a medical school near you and ask whether they have any reduced-fee programs or studies.

How can I get a referral to a mental health professional?

There are many possible referral sources:

Your primary care provider or family doctor
Probably the fastest way to find a therapist is to ask your family doctor for the name of a psychiatrist, psychologist, or other mental health specialist who has a background in treating OCD. If you belong to an HMO, you probably need to visit your regular doctor first in order to secure a referral. Otherwise, many insurance plans will not cover the cost of your care.

The Obsessive-Compulsive Foundation
Write or call for a referral list of therapists in your area who treat obsessive-compulsive disorders. See Appendix A for contact information.)

The Association for Advancement of Behavior Therapy
Most behavior therapists belong to the AABT, which publishes a directory of its members. Write

the AABT to inquire whether a particular therapist is a member and ask also if he or she lists OCD as a specialty. See Appendix A for contact information.

The Anxiety Disorders Association of America

This association can provide referrals to therapists who specialize in anxiety disorders. See Appendix A.

Other professional associations

The American Psychiatric Association and the American Psychological Association can also provide referrals to psychiatrists in your area. Their addresses and phone numbers are listed in Appendix A.

The department of psychiatry at the nearest university medical school

If your town has a university, look in the phone book for the number of the department of psychiatry, and call for a list of referrals. Residents may offer treatment at reduced fees, or there may be an ongoing research study in which treatment is gratis.

The American Medical Association

Call your local branch and request a list of psychiatrists in your area. Be sure to inquire if any of them have particular expertise in OCD and exposure-and-response prevention.

The physician-referral service at your local hospital

A hospital can give you the names of psychiatrists practicing in your community. They may also be able to give you some information about their orientation, background, and training.

The physician-referral service at a private psychiatric facility in your area

Here you may be able to obtain more specific information about psychiatrists with a special focus on OCD. Referrals, however, are usually restricted to doctors on the hospital staff.

A community mental health center

More accessible and affordable than a private hospital, your local health department can steer you toward a community health center that charges fees on a sliding scale, based on your income.

Clergy

Your rabbi, priest, or minister is experienced in coping with the emotional difficulties of his congregation. He can help you get in touch with a religiously affiliated mental health center, such as those sponsored by the Jewish or Catholic Family Services.

A family member who has been treated for OCD

Since OCD tends to run in families, it's very possible that someone else in your family has successfully confronted its challenges. Even if they're not located in your part of the country, they may be able to refer you to an expert in OCD in your area.

A support group

The OC Foundation is a good source for locating support groups, as are local hospitals and health departments. Attend a meeting and get the low-down on OCD care providers in your area. Many support groups are based on twelve-step programs like Alcoholics Anonymous and can greatly help people manage behavior. To find a support group near you, you can also contact:

The American Self-Help Clearinghouse
St. Clares-Riverside Medical Center
Denville, NJ 07034
(973) 625–7101

A school or college

For young people who have OCD, it is probably best for them to approach it hand in hand with their educational institution. Guidance counselors and school social workers can refer you to a mental health professional, and most colleges and universities offer free or low-cost mental health services at clinics on campus.

Should I seek out someone who specializes in obsessive-compulsive disorder and exposure-and-response prevention?

Absolutely. When consulting a mental health professional, it is imperative to ask whether they offer exposure-and-response prevention, for many professionals do not. To confirm that you have made the right choice, ask the therapist some of the following questions:

- Do you practice behavior therapy? (Remember that it is much easier to find a psychiatrist who can prescribe medication than it is to locate a mental health specialist who has experience in exposure-and-response prevention.)

- Do you have experience with anxiety disorders?

- Do you have any special training in OCD?

- What percentage of your practice do you devote to people with OCD? How many people with OCD have you treated? (A therapist who has no experience with OCD is not the right one for you.)

- What is your basic approach to treatment—medication, behavior therapy, or both? If you provide only one of these, how do I obtain the other if I need it? (This is an especially important question for a therapist who is not a psychiatrist, for only psychiatrists can prescribe medication.)

- Do you prescribe medication if it is necessary? (Some very reputable psychiatrists do not recommend medication of any kind, and it is best to know this beforehand.)

- Do you teach, lecture, or write about OCD? (This would be a good sign, indicating up-to-the-minute knowledge and experience in dealing with your problem.)

- Are you licensed by the state? (If the answer is no, you may prefer to look elsewhere.)

- Have other primary care providers referred patients with OCD to you?

- How long is a typical course of treatment?

- How long is each session?

- What is the cost?

- Can you help me determine whether my health insurance covers the cost of my treatment? If it doesn't, do you offer fees on a sliding scale?

- Do you approve of alternative approaches, such as biofeedback or herbal remedies? (This is a good question if you want to supplement your regular treatment. Many mental health specialists are strongly opposed to alternative treatments.)

Is good "chemistry" with my therapist necessary?

It's important to find a therapist who is warm, supportive, understanding, and intelligent. You should feel comfortable enough with your therapist to be open and honest about your thoughts and rituals, hopefully without feeling either foolish or ashamed about them. On the other hand, there's really no need to try to match personalities or interests. The relationship between you and your behavior therapist is in fact less close than one established in more traditional approaches such as psychotherapy.

I've been seeing my therapist for several weeks and I don't feel any better. What should I do?

You must give your therapist time to work on your case. In the case of antiobsessive medication, it can take up to three months for any substantive changes to take effect. Behavior therapy averages ten to twelve weeks and sometimes much longer. Be patient, and don't try to rush results. As long as the therapy makes sense, it's okay to give it some time, even if you don't feel better right away. On the other hand, if it makes no sense at all to you, talk to your therapist about it.

Chapter 6
BEHAVIOR THERAPY

What is behavior therapy?

Behavior therapy, or BT, is a form of psychotherapy that focuses on identifying and changing negative patterns of behavior. It may help to think of behavior therapy as the flip side of cognitive therapy, which focuses on changing negative thought patterns. Substance abuse, alcoholism, and eating disorders—all of which involve abnormal ways of acting—also respond well to BT.

What is the best type of behavior therapy for OCD?

Exposure-and-response prevention is widely considered the best form of behavior therapy for people who have obsessive-compulsive disorders. Its goals are to suppress intrusive urges, calm the anxiety arising from obsessions, and reduce or eliminate rituals. In this book, when we refer to behavior therapy, we mean the exposure-and-response prevention that is most often used to treat OCD.

What is exposure-and-response prevention?

There are two central elements to this technique:

1.   Exposure means openly confronting a situation or object that you fear.
2.   Response prevention means resisting the urge to perform a ritual afterward.

What happens in exposure-and-response prevention?

This very simple and straightforward approach to OCD can result in dramatic improvements. It involves exposing the OCD sufferer to a feared object or situation and then helping him to forgo the usual anxiety-reducing rituals. The idea is to remain in contact with the triggers of distress for gradually longer periods of time without resorting to repetitive compulsive behavior. Eventually your body will learn that fears disappear on their own, even when rituals are not performed, because there is no real basis for the anxiety and nervous apprehension of OCD.

How does behavior therapy help control the fears and rituals typical of OCD?

Exposure-and-response prevention reinforces the knowledge that nothing bad really happens in response to your fears. An obsession is like a false interpretation of real data that in turn sets off a false alarm in your body. Behavior therapy helps you turn off the false alarm.

When you have OCD, the rituals you perform in

response to fears and obsessions reinforce interpretations and ideas that are false or wrong. For example, a definite relationship exists between blood and AIDS, but OCD sufferers often stretch this relationship to unusual and unrealistic extremes. They often believe they will catch AIDS simply from touching public telephones or elevator buttons.

Exposure-and-response prevention helps extinguish false relationships like these by exposing them as unrealistic and untrue. In time, by making these false relationships disappear, behavior therapy keeps the false alarms from going off. In so doing, it gradually enables people who have OCD to gain more control over their symptoms and their lives.

Does this mean I should try to avoid the triggers of my symptoms?

Absolutely not. Your goal in behavior therapy is not to avoid the sources of your anxiety but rather to confront them. When you *don't* follow the triggers with the usual rituals—and nothing bad happens—bit by bit you will learn to tolerate the anxiety of obsessions. For example, if you don't check and recheck that the doors are securely locked, your house will still not be burgled. If you fail to wash your hands after touching a doorknob or a parking meter or public elevator button, you will not get AIDS or cancer.

As you forgo your rituals again and again without any ill consequences, the cumulative effect will be powerful. Over time you will come to fully grasp and believe what you knew intellectually all along: These fears are unreasonable and unfounded. They are part of your disease. When you realize this, your anxiety will recede by increments, and eventually you will succeed in taking back your life from the obsessions and compulsions of OCD.

Is behavior therapy for everyone?

No. In order to succeed, behavior therapy requires your active commitment and participation. If you're not fully committed to the process, it will fail. Exposure-and-response prevention requires a lot of work, and some OCD sufferers are just not up to it. People who have passive personalities would probably rather take a pill, and medication is a better route for them. In addition, those who are depressed usually require medication before they can summon the motivation and energy necessary to succeed with behavior therapy.

What can I expect to happen in my first session with a behavior therapist?

The first step in therapy is evaluation of your symptoms. Initial questions are usually open-ended, to elicit as much information as possible. Your therapist may ask:

- Do you have some thought that occurs over and over again? Tell me about it.
- Do you repeat certain types of behavior? What are some examples?

What happens next?

Your therapist will gradually grow more specific in her queries. Expect her over time to explore your thoughts and rituals in great detail with you. Exactly what rituals do you practice? When do they occur? Just what thoughts and fears appear to trigger them? Specific questions might include:

- Are you overly concerned with cleanliness?
- How many times a day do you wash your hands?
- Do you follow a specific pattern when you wash your hands? For instance, do you wash your fingers in a certain order, followed by fingernails and lastly palms?
- Do you visit the doctor more often than recommended or necessary because you are unreasonably afraid of getting a life-threatening disease such as cancer?
- If your doctor says you are fine, do you see another physician or two just to make sure?
- Are you afraid of catching AIDS from casual contact with harmless objects?
- Are your fears making you a prisoner in your own home? Is it easier to stay in your pajamas

and watch TV than face the "contaminated" world outside?

- Do simple things like getting dressed or taking a shower consume an inordinate amount of your time?
- Do you have trouble making it to work on time and performing your required tasks there?
- Do you perform tasks in a certain order? Does it trouble you when you vary from that sequence in a small way?
- Does it take you a very long time to accomplish a simple task?
- Do you consider yourself an extremely careful person?
- Do you check to make sure the door is locked each time you leave the house?
- How many times do you check the lock?
- Have you ever turned your car around and driven back home to make sure that the door was locked or the gas on the stove was turned off?
- Do you check the plugs on electrical appliances?
- How many other things do you check?
- Are you unduly worried about the safety of yourself or others?
- Do you have doubts about your own observations and perceptions?
- Do you constantly seek reassurance from family and friends that all is well? That you haven't inadvertently insulted or hurt them?

- Do you repeat yourself a lot?
- Do you apologize over and over for small and perhaps even nonexistent slights?
- Are you afraid that you might have hit a pedestrian with your car or caused a traffic accident?
- Do you pick up items from the trash?
- Is your home filled with old newspapers or boxes or jars that may come in handy someday?
- Do you repeat little phrases or count certain sequences of numbers to prevent bad things from happening?
- Do you have superstitions about colors or numbers?
- Are you unduly upset when someone disturbs the order of books on your office shelves or soups in your kitchen closet?
- Do you have distressing thoughts of a pornographic, violent, or blasphemous nature? Even though you despise these thoughts, do you find yourself unable to control them?

My therapist and I have identified my obsessions and compulsions. What happens next?

Once you have clearly identified your problems, it's time to work with your therapist to establish specific goals for treatment. Precisely what do you want to accomplish? For example, if you wash your hands fifty times a day, your ultimate goal would be to wash them only as needed. Since you may no longer be sure of what's necessary and what is excessive, ask your therapist to help you spell this out. Make a list. For instance, it's reasonable to wash after using the bathroom and before preparing or eating meals. It's sensible to clean your hands after gardening or changing the baby or taking out the garbage. But when you feel a need to bathe after shaking hands with a business colleague or purchasing a newspaper at a public newsstand, that's your OCD talking. In behavior therapy you will learn to distinguish between normal needs and urges and those brought on by your disease.

How do I reach my ultimate goal in therapy?

Behavior therapy is a gradual process. In addition to your long-term goal, it's vital to establish a series of short-term goals to strive toward along the way. After all, you can't go from fifty washes a day to nine or ten without making some stops in between. So this week try to wash only forty times a day, next week make it thirty times, until bit by bit you work your way to your ultimate goal. Don't allow yourself to become discouraged by expecting too much too soon.

What specific techniques might my therapist use to help me reach my goals?

Graded desensitization and flooding are two very helpful techniques for treating OCD. In graded desensitization you tackle your fears one by one, beginning with the least anxiety-provoking and gradually working your way up to the most distressing and anxiety-provoking obsession. Flooding takes an opposite approach, in which the OCD sufferer is confronted and flooded all at once with the very thing he fears the most.

How does graded desensitization work?

Your therapist will probably begin by asking you to make a list of all the things you fear. Next you will rate these fears on a scale according to how much or how little anxiety you feel when experiencing them.

Start with a short and simple exercise. Say that you have contamination fears. Perhaps you are terrified of germs and can't bear to use the towels in public rest rooms. Your therapist might begin by working with you on a regular basis to lightly touch a soiled towel in the safe environment of her office. Next you might pick up the towel and hold it in your hand. In each session of behavior therapy, you would hold the soiled towel for a longer period. Hold it five minutes, then ten minutes, then twenty. Gradually build it up.

As you touch and hold the very thing you fear— without performing the usual follow-up ritual— and nothing bad happens, in time you will conquer your fear. Finally you might use a towel in a public rest room. After you have achieved this short-term goal in the process of graded desensitization, you will move on to confronting your next most anxiety-provoking fear.

What is flooding like?

Unlike graded desensitization, flooding immediately confronts you with your most feared obsession. It always takes place in the safe and secure environment of your therapist's office. There, if you are afraid of AIDS, you may be asked to hold a handkerchief with blood on it and forgo washing your hands. Then you can sit safely—if anxiously—in your doctor's office as you eventually come to the realization that nothing bad will happen to you in consequence of this action.

I've just started practicing exposure-and-response prevention, and I feel more anxious than ever. What should I do?

Not surprisingly, many people grow even more uncomfortable and anxious than usual in the initial stages of behavior therapy. They often experience a short-term increase in their obsessions and urges to ritualize. But don't allow yourself to become discouraged: This stage will pass. If like most people you can tolerate a temporary increase in symptoms, over the long term there will be less discomfort and a decrease in intrusive obsessions and compulsions. Keep in mind that medication can be particularly helpful in controlling temporary increases in anxiety levels, characteristic of early stages of behavior therapy.

What are some typical goals of behavior therapy?

Broadly speaking, the ultimate goal of all OCD sufferers is to eliminate or at least significantly reduce the intrusive thoughts and repetitive behaviors that are so distressing and that prevent them from living normal lives. But the individual goals vary greatly from person to person. They may include:

- If you're concerned that something bad will happen if you leave your house open, your goal is to check once only that the doors are locked.

- If you believe that you may accidentally burn your house down by leaving an appliance on, your goal is to check just once to make sure that the electrical plugs and switches are turned off.

- If you fear that your car is going to roll down a hill and hurt someone, your goal is to check the emergency brake only once.

- If you have persistent thoughts that you have hit someone with your car, your goal is to resist the urge to drive over the same patch of road again and again to make sure that all is well.

- If your problem is with hoarding, your goal is to allow yourself to pick up only one piece of trash and eventually to stop picking up rubbish altogether.

- If your impulse is to enter your house according to an elaborate set of rituals, your goal is to resist it.

- If you collect so much junk that you can no longer walk around your crowded house, your goal is to fill several garbage bags with odds and ends each week and dispose of them, and throw out all your old newspapers.

- If arranging items into symmetrical patterns is consuming the hours of your day, your goal is to refrain from doing it.
- If you think that you must ward off disaster by putting on your right shoe before your left, your goal is to be able to reverse it.

Once you see that nothing bad happens when you violate your old patterns, you will begin to break the tyranny of your obsessions and compulsions.

It's easy to say "just resist your urges." But anyone who has OCD knows how painfully difficult it really is. Exactly how does behavior therapy help me control my rituals?

Here's an example. If your obsession centers on contamination, you may see germs and bacteria everywhere. Consequently, you become very anxious when you touch a germ-laden doorknob, a bacteria-ridden public telephone, an electric light switch, or a newspaper. Shaking hands with people and using public rest rooms can be very threatening experiences. To an OCD sufferer, the only way to relieve the anxiety brought on by these contamination fears seems to be to wash and wash again.

Exposure-and-response prevention offers a better alternative. In this type of behavior therapy, you would define your long-term goal as washing only when appropriate. In order to accomplish this

long-term goal, your short-term goal would be to
overcome individual fears of contamination one by
one. For example, this week touch a doorknob and
don't wash your hands for five minutes. Next week
touch a doorknob and don't wash for fifteen minutes. Once you have mastered doorknobs, do the
same with telephones, light switches, and so on.
When you are ready, your therapist might shake
hands with you and ask you not to wash until the
session is over. Eventually you will work your way
up to using public rest rooms.

The concept of behavior therapy is to deliberately take on each fear one at a time. Confront it,
conquer it, and move on. Touch all these "contaminated" things and then *don't* wash your hands or
take a shower, and see that nothing bad happens in
consequence. You will not become ill with some
dreadful disease. No harm will befall you or your
loved ones because you do not perform cleansing
or other rituals. As this outcome becomes increasingly clear, your anxiety will retreat. Obsessions
and compulsions may eventually disappear altogether, although more likely they will fade into the
background so they no longer interfere so much in
your day-to-day life.

**What if I can manage to replace a cleansing or
checking ritual with a counting ritual in my head?
Is that a good thing?**

No. Although this substitution may at first appeal
to you because it will help hide your symptoms, it's

completely counterproductive to your treatment. If you relieve your anxiety by simply replacing physical rituals with mental ones, you're not making any progress. If instead of checking the lock, you count back and forth to one hundred, you're on the wrong track. In fact, you might well end up making matters worse by extending the pattern of your compulsions.

How will my therapist help me achieve my goals?

You and your therapist will work together very closely to design a program to help you face your specific fears. Although there are common elements in obsessions and compulsions, each person's program is unique to their particular experience of OCD. It is essential to identify your personal triggers of obsessions, compulsions, and anxiety.

What are examples of individualized treatment programs?

Some people with OCD agonize about catching AIDS as they accept change from the hand of a grocery store clerk or are served dinner by a waiter. A long-term goal for someone with this problem might be to eat out in a restaurant or shop for groceries without being overcome by fears of contamination. In order to get to this point, a short-term achievement could be to visit a hospice and see that you can't get AIDS from casual contact with someone who definitely has the disease.

If you have overwhelming fears of harming

yourself or your family, you probably shun contact with others and avoid all sharp objects such as knives and scissors. Your ultimate goal might be to hug your wife or to cook a meal or do a crafts project with your child without experiencing intense anxieties about hurting them. If you're afraid of harming your wife, a short-term achievement would be to gently put your hands on her neck and see that nothing bad happens. Do this at first just for a moment or two, then for increasing lengths of time. You will not hurt her. As you see that no harm comes from this, you will begin to control your fears of harming yourself, your family, and others.

How long is each behavior therapy session?

Sessions with your therapist generally last a little under an hour. This is the minimum amount of time required for exposure-and-response prevention to be successful. When you practice with a buddy, it's a good idea to work at it for even longer, perhaps for an hour or two. If you stay in a threatening situation for this period of time without performing your ritual, you will learn that anxiety eventually subsides on its own as you begin to feel better without giving in to your urges.

Is it a good idea to ask a friend or family member to help me practice exposure-and-response prevention?

Absolutely. It is important that they do so for at least two reasons. First of all, it's very common for people with OCD to become isolated from their loved ones. Don't let this happen to you. Isolation leads to depression and other emotional problems.

Second, a spouse or close friend can help you by encouraging you to resist your urges. In addition to the sessions with your therapist, set aside specific times to meet with this person to practice exposure-and-response prevention.

How should I go about choosing someone to help me with behavior therapy?

Select someone whom you love and trust, and with whom you can openly and honestly share your experiences of OCD. Tell him all about your long- and short-term goals. The right person should be strong enough to keep you honest and not let you give in to urges or simply replace one ritual with another. But you also don't want someone who is overly critical and judgmental about your doubts and fears and questions. By this time, you may have lost track of what's appropriate and what's not. If you don't know whether it is reasonable to shower after using a public rest room, you should feel comfortable asking your helper. When you meet with success in reaching a short-term goal, your helper should be there to praise you. When you become discouraged at the slow pace of improvement, he should be there to buck you up.

Can my helper let me know when there's no real reason for my anxiety? That way I won't feel compelled to perform the usual ritual.

No. Don't let your helper fall into the enabling trap of reassurance. It's not his job to tell you that everything's okay and that you don't need to perform your ritual. As difficult as it is, you must come to this realization on your own.

How many months does behavior therapy usually last?

Behavior therapy is a focused, time-limited treatment. Yet its length varies greatly from individual to individual. If your symptoms are mild, treatment may require only ten to twelve sessions. In severe cases, a year or more of therapy may be necessary.

Is behavior therapy equally effective in controlling all types of compulsive behavior?

People who have cleaning and checking compulsions appear to derive the most benefits from behavior therapy. Fortunately, these are by far the most common rituals. Those who engage in less common OCD behaviors, such as hoarding, repeating rituals, counting compulsions, compulsive slowness, and symmetry obsessions, may not get quite as much out of behavior therapy. Yet while all rituals are not equally responsive to treatment, behavior therapy may still be helpful to some extent. It may just take a little more time and effort on your part.

When was behavior therapy first applied to OCD?

Exposure-and-response behavior therapy for OCD was first developed in the 1960s, when little effective treatment for OCD was available.

I've heard of a technique called thought stopping. Is that useful?

Thought stopping is a good therapeutic technique to use against mental rituals. Since obsessive thoughts of perverse sex or violence are not logical or realistic, you cannot reason them away. It's best to simply close the door to these disturbing thoughts. Your therapist may have you practice doing this in her office by shouting "Stop!" You can also practice at home. Eventually you will come to the point where you can visualize yourself shouting stop, or perhaps whisper it or mouth it under your breath. At the same time it may be helpful to picture a door slamming or a big red and white stop sign.

What happens when my behavior therapy sessions are complete?

To hold on to the gains you made during therapy, pay attention to your lifestyle. Most importantly, control the level of stress in your life. Get a good balance of rest and exercise. Exercise is a particularly good way to relieve stress and anxiety.

Think of behavior therapy as a kind of inoculation against OCD, after which it is normal to need periodic booster shots. If you find yourself once more washing your hands too frequently or avoiding certain places and situations because of obsessive fears, make an appointment to see your therapist. Many people with OCD also attend monthly or even weekly support groups with others who suffer from this disease. As you watch others successfully coping with their fears, it may help you control your own.

Is behavior therapy alone the most effective treatment program for OCD?

For people who suffer from severe OCD, the best treatment is very often a combination of exposure-and-response prevention along with medication with serotonin-reuptake inhibitors. Milder cases of OCD usually respond well to behavior therapy alone.

Are behavior therapy and medication equally effective treatments for OCD?

Interestingly, used separately, behavior therapy and medication have roughly the same rates of success. Although no studies confirm this, it's probable that a combination of medication and therapy is best in very troublesome cases. The long-term outcome is almost always better when behavior therapy plays some role in treatment. Medication alone will probably not reduce the likelihood of future episodes, but the lessons learned in behavior therapy can help keep you from lapsing back into obsessive-compulsive patterns when under stress.

Should behavior therapy always be accompanied by medication in severe cases of OCD?

Not necessarily. This is an important decision that you must make in consultation with your doctor. But in severe cases behavior therapy is more manageable after medication has lessened the intense anxiety brought on by very intrusive thoughts and demanding rituals. Keep in mind that drug treatment does not usually cause significant side effects.

What if I suffer from mild OCD? Do I still need to take medication along with behavior therapy?

Probably not. Although medication might be helpful, in mild cases of OCD behavior therapy alone is often sufficient to control symptoms.

What if I suffer from other emotional problems in addition to OCD?

This combination is very common, as the anxiety and emotional trauma of coping with obsessions and compulsions lead to depression in one out of every two people who have OCD. If you are depressed, it is hard to focus and to summon the motivation to participate in behavior therapy. In order to tolerate the anxiety caused by exposure-and-response prevention, you may need to take medication first to control your depression or other emotional problems.

What are the advantages of behavior therapy over medication?

There are several advantages:

- Behavior therapy is especially appealing to the many OCD sufferers who can't or don't want to take medication. A small number of people who have contamination fears are also unwilling to take medication because they view it as a contaminant.

- Unlike drugs, behavior therapy has no side effects. Moreover, not everyone who has OCD responds to drug therapy with antiobsessive medications.

- Perhaps most important, behavior therapy has more lasting benefits than medication. When most people stop taking medication, their symptoms return. The results of exposure-and-response prevention can be better maintained once therapy is over. When you are under stress, you can practice exposure-and-response prevention to prevent symptoms from recurring.

Does medication have any advantage over behavior therapy?

Taking a pill is always easier than making a commitment to behavior therapy, which can be very hard work. This is especially true in the beginning of therapy, when most OCD sufferers find it extremely frightening to resist the rituals that ordinarily give them relief from the intense pain of their obsessions.

Why is a combination of behavior therapy and medication often best?

Experts agree that medication can take the edge off severe OCD symptoms and allow patients to focus more clearly on therapy. Dr. Jeffrey Schwartz, the author of *Brain Lock*—which offers a four-step program of self-directed behavior therapy to overcome OCD—likens medication to "water wings."

Water wings reduce your child's fear and help him float while he is learning to swim. Likewise, according to Dr. Schwartz, in the early stages of his therapy program, one-half to two-thirds of OCD sufferers find that medication suppresses intrusive urges and lessens anxiety levels, allowing them to concentrate on the therapy that will help them change their brain chemistry and conquer OCD. The analogy continues, because as children learn to swim, they are less and less dependent on their water wings. As therapy progresses, many people with OCD continue taking medication while others reduce or eliminate their dosages.

Is there any scientific evidence that behavior therapy works?

Both behavior therapy conducted by a therapist and self-directed behavior therapy cause positive changes in the brain chemistry of people who have OCD. Using sophisticated imaging techniques, scientists have shown that brain structures that are abnormal in OCD sufferers operate normally after they change their behavior.

Researchers have used positron-emission tomography (PET scans) to show that four parts of the brain—the orbital cortex, caudate nucleus, cingulate gyrus, and thalamus—grow abnormally hyperactive when people who have OCD actively experience symptoms. These four brain parts appear to become locked together in a frantic pattern of firing off inaccurate distress signals to one another. Scientists including Dr. Schwartz speculate that this tight and hyperactive linkage—which he calls "brain lock"—may be the cause of OCD.

In patients who respond to therapy, PET scans show that high metabolic levels of activity drop off and the four parts of the brain begin to operate more independently of one another once more. Researchers theorize that as a person learns to tolerate the disturbing messages his brain receives and changes his response to them, he somehow changes his brain chemistry.

Will behavior therapy eliminate all my OCD problems?

OCD is a chronic problem, and even when you receive the best treatment possible, complete elimination of all symptoms is highly unlikely.

Does behavior therapy work for everyone?

Unfortunately, no. It's helpful to have realistic expectations. Certain symptoms respond better than others to behavior therapy. For example, it is not very effective in treating pure obsessions. In addition, behavior therapy is less successful in those who have both OCD and other psychological problems such as depression.

Is it important to involve my family in treatment?

When OCD behavior disrupts family relations, it's a very good idea to involve family members. Sometimes spouses or parents unwittingly support rituals and, despite the best of intentions, undermine treatment. For example, if you bleach all the clothes or wash the floor with ammonia to ease your spouse's contamination fears, you are helping him give in to his urges by performing his rituals for him. (Read more about OCD and the family in Chapter 9.)

Whom should I consult for behavior therapy?

Therapy can be very difficult and painful for you and for your family. This is why it's best to consult a mental health professional with specific training in exposure-and-response prevention. Contact the

Obsessive-Compulsive Foundation (OCF) at (203) 878–5669 for a list of behavior therapists. (For more tips about how to locate a therapist, turn to Chapter 5.)

Will my health insurance cover behavior therapy?

Coverage depends on the type of insurance you have and your diagnosis. Health plans tend to make a distinction between physical and mental illness, and coverage for mental illness is far more restrictive. Many plans limit the number of mental health visits you are allowed in a year and place a lifetime cap on mental health costs. Copayments for individual visits are also greater. Unfortunately, most health plans do not take into account the fact that mental illnesses such as OCD have biochemical causes.

What should I do if my insurance company doesn't cover the cost of behavior therapy?

OCD is a serious problem. You owe it to yourself to address your illness regardless of the cost. When possible, pay for the treatment yourself. If this is a hardship, find a therapist who offers fees on a sliding scale (a discount for those who cannot afford the full amount).

Do any other kinds of psychotherapy help in treating OCD?

Behavior therapy is the only psychological approach that has been shown to be consistently effective in treating OCD. Techniques such as cognitive therapy, psychoanalysis, and psychotherapy don't appear to have any impact on this disease. They may, however, help you deal with stress, which can trigger obsessive-compulsive symptoms, and with accompanying problems such as depression.

Is my therapy different if I have other emotional problems in addition to OCD?

Yes. Cognitive behavior therapy, group therapy, and self-help groups may be helpful when OCD is accompanied by depression, anxiety, or other problems.

I'm not sure how severe my OCD is. Should I try behavior therapy alone? Or should I combine therapy with medication?

Behavior therapy and medication with serotonin-reuptake inhibitors are the two most effective modes of treatment for OCD. The decision about which therapy is right for you is a very individual one, best made after careful consideration and discussion with your doctor.

Behavior therapy is a challenging process. Exposure to the situations you fear may seem almost unbearable to you, especially at first. Holding a dirty towel or using a public rest room—without gaining any relief by repeatedly washing afterward—is probably the last thing in this world you want to do. Although you may intellectually understand this exercise and recognize that it is to your benefit in the long run, it can be quite painful at the time. Yet behavior therapy can help control your symptoms, and it has a long-lasting impact even when treatment is over. When you are under stress and whenever you feel the pull of rituals slipping back into your life, you can practice the techniques of exposure-and-response prevention to get yourself back on the right track. As you will learn in the next chapter, antiobsessive medications can also help control your OCD symptoms.

Chapter 7

ANTIOBSESSIVE MEDICATIONS

What are the best medications for obsessive-compulsive disorder?

Drugs that regulate the neurotransmitter serotonin are far and away the best choice for OCD. Research strongly suggests that serotonin plays a central role in obsessive-compulsive disorder, and thus the recent introduction of selective serotonin-reuptake inhibitors (antidepressants that are also known as SSRIs) has revolutionized the treatment of this disease. In fact, scientists now believe that *only* drugs that affect serotonin are effective in controlling the symptoms of OCD.

What is an antidepressant?

An antidepressant is a prescription drug designed to relieve the symptoms of depression by changing the function and structure of brain tissue. Certain antidepressants—specifically, the tricyclic antidepressant clomipramine and the SSRIs—also help control obsessive-compulsive symptoms.

Unlike addictive drugs such as tranquilizers and opioids, antidepressants have little potential for drug abuse. In people who suffer from depression and OCD, they correct the abnormal actions of neurotransmitters in the brain. Over time the regular use of medication can suppress the intensity of intrusive urges and rituals, as well as lift black moods and other symptoms of depression.

What are neurotransmitters?

Neurotransmitters such as serotonin are vital chemicals that carry messages from nerve cell to nerve cell in the brain. In addition to serotonin, the neurotransmitter most closely associated with OCD, other neurotransmitters are norepinephrine and dopamine. When an imbalance in these chemical messengers occurs, emotional and physical symptoms can result.

What is serotonin?

Serotonin is an important neurotransmitter that has a distinct impact on a wide variety of brain activities, including behavior, mood, appetite, sexual activity, hormone secretion, movement, and heart rate. Serotonin can be looked on as the brain's own natural antidepressant and tranquilizer. When you're experiencing obsessive-compulsive symptoms, there's an imbalance of serotonin in the brain.

How do antiobsessive drugs work?

Antiobsessive medications gradually reduce the intensity of disturbing thoughts and rituals by ensuring that the brain has a sufficient amount of serotonin. Serotonin and other neurotransmitters are absolutely essential to communication among brain cells.

To understand antiobsessive drugs, it's necessary to know a little bit about how your brain works. Your behavior, mood, and emotions are a result of communication among cells in your brain. Nerve cells, or neurons, communicate with one another via chemical messengers called neurotransmitters, which travel from nerve cell to nerve cell across spaces called synapses. Having crossed a synapse, neurotransmitters pass along messages about moods and emotions by attaching themselves to receptors on neighboring nerve cells.

A communications snafu occurs when serotonin is lost somewhere in this process. In the brains of people with OCD, serotonin seems to be sucked back into nerve cells instead of advancing across the synapse. Valuable chemical messages get lost, and OCD symptoms result. The problem seems to be not merely that there is not enough serotonin, but that there are shortages in particular locations. Just where all these locations are is something that scientists are continuing to look into.

Antiobsessive drugs such as SSRIs work by selectively blocking the absorption, or "reuptake," of serotonin in the area of the receptors. Hence their complicated name: selective serotonin-reuptake inhibitors. Basically, antiobsessive medications make sure that enough serotonin remains available in the synapses between nerve fibers (instead of being reabsorbed into nerve cells), so that more serotonin can attach itself to serotonin receptors on adjacent nerve cells. The flow of nerve impulses returns to normal, and messages are passed along more efficiently among the various nerve cells in the brain.

Can antiobsessive medications help everyone with OCD?

Unfortunately, no. While medications can be very helpful, they are no "magic bullet." Drug therapy helps four to six out of every ten people with OCD, and while symptoms are reduced in these cases, they are rarely eliminated completely. Studies generally show that medication reduces the severity of OCD symptoms by 25 to 35 percent, as measured by the Yale-Brown Obsessive Compulsive Scale (Y-BOCS). On the positive side, this is often enough relief to allow people to function at a less anxious, more normal level. And since medication takes the edge off the intensity of thoughts and compulsions, it sets the stage for the next recommended stage of treatment: behavior therapy.

When were effective medications for OCD first developed?

Clomipramine, the most widely studied drug for OCD, was the first medication to raise levels of serotonin and thus have a significant impact on OCD. Although developed in the 1970s in Europe, clomipramine—a tricyclic antidepressant whose brand name is Anafranil—was not approved for OCD treatment in the United States until 1990. Before that time, however, it had been prescribed for OCD as an "off-label" use. Clomipramine has a good safety record, having been used in dozens of countries around the world for two decades.

What does "off-label" use mean?

Pharmaceutical companies typically apply to the FDA for approval of a drug to treat one medical problem at a time. But once the FDA has approved, or labeled, that drug as safe for the original symptom or disease, it may have other uses as well. The pharmaceutical company will likely apply for approval to treat these other conditions, but it may take months or even years. In the meantime doctors routinely prescribe drugs on an off-label basis. Although clomipramine was originally approved for the treatment of depression, it was also an effective treatment for OCD and was prescribed for OCD on an off-label basis.

When did SSRIs come on the market?

The first selective serotonin-reuptake inhibitor was Prozac (fluoxetine), which hit the antidepressant market with a bang in 1988. At the time no one (including maker Eli Lilly & Company) predicted the dramatic impact Prozac would have on the world. But Prozac and the other SSRIs that followed were as effective and had fewer side effects than older antidepressants. Today SSRIs control a commanding 96 percent of the antidepressant market, with Prozac accounting for 40 percent of that total.

How many antiobsessive medications are there?

As of now, five antidepressants have been approved by the Food and Drug Administration (FDA) for the treatment of OCD, and more are under development. They include one tricyclic antidepressant and four SSRIs.

Following is a list by category of the major antidepressants for OCD treatment. Drugs are identified by their generic names followed by their brand names:

- Tricyclic Antidepressants
  clomipramine (Anafranil)
- Selective Serotonin-Reuptake Inhibitors
  fluoxetine (Prozac)
  sertraline (Zoloft)
  fluvoxamine (Luvox)
  paroxetine (Paxil)

How will my doctor decide which antiobsessive medication is right for me?

Your doctor will examine the type, severity, and longevity of your OCD symptoms in order to decide on an appropriate treatment. In general, the SSRIs are the first line of attack against OCD. Although clomipramine may be a tiny bit more effective than the SSRIs in controlling symptoms, its side effects make it much harder to tolerate. In contrast, SSRIs are very effective and cause few side effects.

What do the different antiobsessive medications have in common with one another?

The tricyclic clomipramine and the four SSRIs—fluoxetine, sertraline, fluvoxamine, and paroxetine—all work by regulating the availability of serotonin in the brain. Specifically, they inhibit serotonin reuptake, or prevent serotonin from being reabsorbed into nerve cells. This makes more serotonin available to receptors on adjacent nerve cells.

How are they different from one another?

SSRIs cause far fewer side effects than does clomipramine. Tricyclic antidepressants such as clomipramine have anticholinergic properties that result in uncomfortable side effects such as dry mouth, constipation, drowsiness, and dizziness.

What exactly is a tricyclic antidepressant?

Tricyclic antidepressants (TCAs) are drugs named for the three rings in their chemical structure. They relieve the symptoms of depression by blocking the reuptake of neurotransmitters in the brain. The only tricyclic antidepressant that has been shown to successfully control obsessive-compulsive symptoms as well as depression is clomipramine (Anafranil).

Why aren't other tricyclic antidepressants also used to treat OCD?

Clomipramine (Anafranil) is indeed very similar to other tricyclic antidepressants, such as amitriptyline (Elavil) and imipramine (Tofranil). Chemically speaking, the only difference between clomipramine and the other tricyclics is one tiny chloride atom. But this atom makes all the difference. Other tricyclics affect norepinephrine only, while clomipramine also has an impact on serotonin levels.

What are the side effects of the tricyclic antidepressant clomipramine?

The side effects of treatment with clomipramine range from mild to severe. Most common are dry mouth, drowsiness, and constipation. A drop in blood pressure may cause you to feel faint if you get up suddenly; this is called postural hypotension. What many people dislike most about clomipramine is that they often gain weight when they take it. Dizziness, blurry vision, loss of sexual desire, delayed orgasms, impotence, excessive sweating, tremors, and heart palpitations have also occurred, and at high dosages (usually over 250 milligrams a day) there have been reports of seizures.

Whenever you experience uncomfortable or certainly dangerous side effects, speak to your therapist. Some problems fade on their own over time, while in other cases your doctor may lower your dose. It may also prove helpful to take the medication at bedtime.

What is a selective serotonin-reuptake inhibitor?

SSRIs, the newest and most dominant class of antidepressants on the market, regulate the levels of the neurotransmitter serotonin in your brain. Since OCD is thought to be caused by a chemical imbalance of serotonin, SSRIs are particularly well suited to controlling the symptoms of OCD. A great advantage of SSRIs is that they cause far fewer side effects than do clomipramine and other older types of antidepressants.

How do SSRIs work?

SSRIs prevent the reuptake (or reabsorption) of the neurotransmitter serotonin, allowing more serotonin to remain available in synapses, the spaces between the nerve cells. This means that serotonin can attach more efficiently to receptors in nearby nerve membranes, and that messages about behavior and emotion can be sent and received more efficiently from one nerve cell to another.

Do SSRIs have any advantages over other antidepressants?

A major advantage is that SSRIs have minimal side effects in comparison with other antidepressants. Yet this is not to say that the side effects of SSRIs—especially the sexual problems—cannot be very disturbing.

Why do SSRIs cause fewer side effects than other antidepressants?

Older tricyclic antidepressants have anticholinergic properties that result in myriad side effects ranging from dry mouth and dizziness to tremors and heart palpitations.

What are the side effects of SSRIs?

Although the side effects of SSRIs are fewer than those of tricyclic antidepressants, they can nonetheless be troubling. Most people consider sexual problems their most worrisome adverse effect. Other common side effects are nausea, diarrhea, headaches, anxiety and nervousness, insomnia or conversely drowsiness, sweating, and heartburn.

As with any medication, be sure to speak with your therapist when you experience uncomfortable side effects. Some problems resolve themselves over time, while others require an adjustment in dosage by your doctor. In many cases taking medication with meals or at bedtime is helpful.

What kinds of sexual problems can be caused by antiobsessive medications?

Many people who take an SSRI experience some kind of sexual side effect. Sexual dysfunction as a result of SSRIs affects both men and women and can include decreased sexual desire, slowed ejaculation, and delayed orgasm. In some cases there is a complete inability to reach orgasm. Many of those who take clomipramine experience these same side effects.

Is there anything I can do to alleviate the sexual side effects of SSRIs and clomipramine?

There are a number of ways to get around disturbing sexual side effects. A good diet, vitamin and mineral supplementation, exercise, stress reduction, adequate rest, and time for lovemaking will go far to increase sexual vitality. It may also be possible to find a medication or dosage level that keeps sexual problems to a minimum. Failing that, ask your doctor or therapist if you can periodically skip your medication; this should restore normal sexual function for that time.

Other drugs taken in combination with SSRIs may be helpful. Ask your doctor about cyproheptadine (Periactin), a drug that temporarily blocks the effects of serotonin. The drugs yohimbine and cyproheptadine may reduce sexual side effects. Some have found the herb ginkgo helpful. (Read more about this herb in Chapter 8.) Of course, anything you take—whether prescription or over-the-counter or herbal—should be carefully reviewed first by your doctor. Like SSRIs, these substances can have serious side effects and interactions.

Most important, be open and honest about your sexual concerns with both your therapist and your significant other. For example, if your therapist fails to ask you about sexual side effects you may be experiencing, don't be shy about bringing them up yourself. When drugs alleviate your symptoms but reduce your sexual desire, let your partner know that it's the chemicals—not you, and not he or she—that are responsible.

What measures can I take to lessen some of the other side effects of antiobsessive medications?

Here are some steps you can try:

• To control diarrhea, avoid greasy and spicy items, and eat binding foods such as rice and bananas. Avoid dairy products, and drink lots of fluids with electrolytes (such as herbal teas, vegetable broths, and electrolyte replacement drinks). Eat a cup of plain yogurt or consider taking a lactobacillus acidophilus supplement to restore the normal balance of intestinal bacteria.

• To relieve constipation, increase your dietary fiber by eating plenty of fresh fruits and vegetables. Drink at least eight glasses of water a day, and make sure you squeeze in regular physical exercise for at least half an hour at a time three days a week.

• To prevent weight gain, pay attention to diet and exercise.

• To relieve dry mouth, drink lots of water and suck on sugar-free hard candies. Over-the-counter preparations such as Saliva Substitute can help, and if nothing else does the trick, your doctor can prescribe Salogen, a drug to promote saliva flow.

• To soothe dull headaches, take over-the-counter analgesics. Relaxation therapy and massage are also helpful, as are calcium and magnesium supplements to increase muscle relaxation.

• If you become faint when you stand up quickly, be aware of this and take your time getting up. Increase your fluids, and eat salty foods to keep your blood pressure up.

• To compensate for blurred vision, take care driving (especially at night), and hold reading material a little farther from your eyes than usual.

• If medication makes you drowsy or sleepy, do not drive or operate machinery until you are fully alert.

• If you suffer from insomnia, make sure you create a good sleep environment with a comfortable bed and a supportive pillow in a dark and quiet bedroom. If irritating noise is a problem, invest in a white noise generator, a water fountain, or nature tapes. To establish normal sleep rhythms, go to bed and get up at the same time, and in the hour before you go to sleep, avoid stimulants such as the TV, the computer, and bright lights. Get regular exercise, and avoid caffeine and alcohol in the evening.

Will I experience the side effects of medications before they begin to control my obsessive-compulsive symptoms?

In all likelihood, yes. It can take as long as ten to twelve weeks for medications to have an impact on OCD. In the meantime, as you cope with uncomfortable side effects, keep in mind that disturbing thoughts and compulsions are far more upsetting and difficult to control than the side effects of the drugs designed to help you get a grip on them.

Will the side effects get better or worse over time?

Unfortunately, there is no way to predict this. Some side effects fade with time, but others do not.

What happens if I can't tolerate the side effects of an antiobsessive medication?

Five different medications are available to control OCD symptoms, and each one varies slightly in its chemical makeup. If the side effects of one are too uncomfortable or distressing to bear, your doctor can switch you to another that may be more successful.

Given all the adverse side effects, why would anyone want to take antiobsessive drugs?

This all depends on the severity of your OCD. If mild or moderate symptoms do not significantly interfere with your day-to-day life, then you may very well be better off without medication. But if

upsetting and demanding thoughts and rituals consume the hours of your day and have a negative
impact on your relationships and work, it's time to
get help. Severe symptoms can be much more disruptive than the side effects of antiobsessive medications.

What happens if the first medication I take doesn't work?

Because the various antidepressants have slightly
different chemical effects upon the brain, there is
no guarantee that the first medication you try will
work. If a three-month period elapses and you feel
no better, your doctor will start you on another
antiobsessive medication.

Why has the SSRI Prozac received so much more media attention than other medications?

In 1988, after fifteen years of research in this country and long after its approval in Europe, the
blockbuster drug Prozac (fluoxetine) was launched
with great fanfare by the Eli Lilly drug company.
Widely hailed as the new miracle drug, Prozac
quickly made the covers of magazines like *News-
week* and *New York*. People thought of Prozac—a
safe and effective treatment for depression in children as well as adults—as a "happy pill" or "personality pill" that would make even the shyest and
most nervous among us suddenly become the life of
the party or the top salesperson at the firm.

As the pro and con volumes lining the shelves of

your local bookstore can tell you, the enthusiasm for Prozac soon became much more measured. One of the first books that came out in the early 1990s was Peter D. Kramer's *Listening to Prozac,* a positive tribute explaining that Prozac modifies personality as well as treating depression. But this book was quickly followed by *Talking Back to Prozac,* by Peter R. and Ginger Ross Breggin. This book featured the negative side of Prozac, highlighting side effects such as anxiety and sexual dysfunction. It was succeeded by a deluge of negative publicity, and many people became convinced that Prozac was a mind-altering drug that could lead to violent behavior.

A generally more balanced view of Prozac now prevails. It may not be the greatest thing since sliced bread, but neither is it any kind of evil potion. The so-called "mind-altering" aspects of Prozac have been revealed to be its ability to clear chronic symptoms of depression such as low self-esteem, feelings of worthlessness, guilt, pessimism, appetite loss, and loss of interest in sex. It does not alter or transform your personality, but sometimes it might seem that way as it in effect restores you to your old self.

Likewise, the side effects of Prozac are very similar to those of the other SSRIs. They are by and large no better and no worse, and as a group SSRIs cause far fewer side effects than any other antidepressant. Nonetheless, problems such as sexual dysfunction, anxiety, headaches, diarrhea, and insomnia do occur.

Prozac stays in your body for quite a long time, taking more than a month to disappear. Since Prozac interferes with the liver's ability to metabolize certain other drugs, watch out for drug interactions; taking Prozac may heighten the effects of other medication. Because it can cause insomnia, Prozac should be taken in the morning.

Are there special concerns with any of the other SSRIs?

Subtle variations exist among the SSRIs, but basically they all cause the same or similar side effects. The small differences among them are due to the fact that they affect different receptor sites in the brain. This is why one SSRI might help diminish your symptoms when another doesn't, and it is also the reason for relatively minor differences in side effects. The most important thing is to locate the SSRI that helps control your symptoms.

Will taking an antiobsessive medication eliminate all my symptoms?

Probably not. Not everyone responds to antiobsessive medications, and even those who do rarely experience 100 percent improvement. But in most cases a medication can significantly reduce the frequency and intensity of obsessions and compulsions. As the resultant anxiety becomes less overwhelming with medication, add a course of exposure-and-response prevention to your treatment to manage the symptoms even more effectively.

Why is combining drug therapy with behavior therapy often the best approach?

Since drug therapy alone doesn't help everyone, it is especially important to take a long-term view and supplement medication with other treatment strategies. Behavior therapy has proven most effective in this regard.

Should people with OCD always be treated with antiobsessive medications?

Not necessarily. Although antiobsessive drugs are largely safe and effective, many people don't like to take medication of any kind, while others find the side effects troubling. Some people who have contamination fears even consider the pills contaminated and are unable to take them.

For these people, behavior therapy is a good option. In severe cases of OCD, however, it may be very difficult for someone to focus on therapy without at least a very low dose of an antiobsessive medication to take the edge off their anxiety.

What is the typical dosage schedule for antiobsessive drugs?

Most antiobsessive medications are taken once or twice a day. It's important to adhere to your schedule and not skip doses. In order to control OCD symptoms, the level of medication in your bloodstream must be consistent.

When should I take my medication?

Whether you take your medication in the morning or at night depends on whether it has a stimulating or sedating side effect. In general, SSRIs have a stimulating effect at the beginning of treatment, but they become more sedating over time. When this happens, change the time of day you take your pill.

More specifically, take Prozac in the morning, because it can cause insomnia; and take Luvox at bedtime, because it can be more sedating than other SSRIs. Since most antiobsessive medications can lead to gastrointestinal distress, be sure to take them with meals or light bedtime snacks.

What happens if I miss a dose?

Missing one dose is not likely to bring about a return of severe symptoms, but missing repeated doses can lead to a problem. If you take the medication several times a day and miss one dose, you can probably add it to your evening dose. But always be sure to check with your doctor first.

How long must I take an antiobsessive medication before I begin to feel better?

This varies according to both the medication itself and the individual taking it, but as a general rule of thumb, you must give each medication at least three months to take full effect. Although these drugs are the same ones used to treat depression, it takes approximately twice as long for them to have an impact on OCD. Interestingly, dosages of antidepressants for OCD are also typically greater than those for depression.

Smaller incremental improvements may be felt before you reach the three-month mark. Generally it takes a minimum of two weeks for any antiobsessive medication to kick in. When a medication appears to work any earlier than this, it is probably due to a placebo effect.

Why doesn't the medication alleviate my symptoms any faster?

It takes time for drugs to have an impact on long-ingrained patterns of communication within the brain. In addition, slow-acting antidepressants are first administered at a low dose. Your therapist will then gradually increase your dosage until the medication begins to have an impact on OCD symptoms.

What happens if I take an antiobsessive medication for several months and there is no difference in my symptoms?

If you have given a medication a three-month trial and still experience no reduction in OCD symptoms, your therapist will probably increase your dosage or prescribe an alternative antiobsessive drug. Before switching medications, however, you will have to wait a few weeks to allow the first medication to "wash out." Otherwise too much serotonin can accumulate in your system. This can cause a life-threatening stroke or lead to "serotonin syndrome." The symptoms of serotonin syndrome include agitation, confusion, tremors, and muscle spasms.

What other drugs might my doctor prescribe for OCD in combination with an antiobsessive medication?

Since OCD often proves resistant to treatment with clomipramine or an SSRI alone, your doctor may prescribe combination drug therapy. There may be a period of trial and error before your doctor lands on the right combination, if indeed she does. Remember that medication is not effective for everyone with OCD.

One very common combination is Klonopin (or clonazepam) and an SSRI. A benzodiazepine such as Klonopin can help you cope with the overwhelming anxiety of OCD. Another option is to add lithium (a mood stabilizer) or buspirone (a nonaddictive antianxiety drug) to antiobsessive treatment. But while some individuals have experienced relief from these two combinations, as of this writing there are no controlled studies to confirm that they work.

For those who suffer from the motor and vocal tics of Tourette's syndrome in addition to OCD, a 1990 study at Yale University showed that adding the drug pimozide to treatment with fluvoxamine (Luvox) reduced the severity of OCD symptoms.

The medication haloperidol has also been shown to be useful in this regard. But both pimozide and haloperidol can have very serious side effects when used for long periods of time, and should be treated with caution.

Once my symptoms are more or less under control, do I still need to keep taking medication?

Since this varies from person to person, it is a question to take up with your therapist. For the vast majority of people, however, if you were taking medication alone, the symptoms will return. While some people are able to stop taking medication after six to twelve months, others must remain on at least low dosages for many years.

If you combine medication with behavior therapy, you have a much better shot at controlling OCD symptoms. Whenever you stop taking a medication, you may reduce your risk of relapse if you learn to control your obsessions and compulsions with behavior therapy techniques as well as drugs.

Should I take medication only when I am under stress and experiencing OCD symptoms?

No. In order for an antiobsessive drug to work, you must take it on a regular basis to maintain a constant level in your bloodstream.

What happens when an antiobsessive medication is discontinued?

If you abruptly stop taking your medication, your obsessive-compulsive symptoms will most likely return. This is why it is vital to stick closely to the treatment plan agreed upon by you and your therapist. Backing up your medication with behavior therapy can also be helpful.

Will I have withdrawal symptoms when I stop taking my medication?

It's possible. This is why it is important to stop taking an antiobsessive medication very slowly. An abrupt cessation can lead to a number of uncomfortable symptoms. In the case of SSRIs, these can include flulike feelings and dizziness. One advantage of Prozac is that it is long-acting, meaning it remains in your body longer than other SSRIs and so is less likely to cause withdrawal symptoms. An abrupt withdrawal from clomipramine can lead to nausea, vomiting, and dizziness.

Were any other drugs ever prescribed to treat OCD?

Absolutely. Remember that a clear understanding of OCD has emerged only in the last ten years or so. Before this time there were no known antiobsessive medications, and therapists prescribed a number of other drugs in a futile attempt to control obsessive-compulsive symptoms. Since depression and anxiety often accompany OCD, these frequently included a variety of antidepressants and antianxiety agents. Yet although they might have helped with accompanying disorders, these medications could not touch the core obsessive-compulsive disorder. Only drugs that specifically affect the neurotransmitter serotonin can control the symptoms of OCD.

Are any other antidepressants prescribed to treat OCD today?

For the most part, no. Since this disease is specifically related to an imbalance in serotonin levels, only medications that affect serotonin have an impact on obsessive-compulsive symptoms. If you suffer from both OCD and depression (the most common complication of OCD), ideally the same drug will be used to treat both conditions. In fact, one of the great benefits of drug therapy for OCD is that the same medications you take for OCD also treat depression. Although it is remotely possible that your doctor may prescribe an SSRI for OCD along with another antidepressant, because of dangerous interactions this must be managed with great care. For example, SSRIs and MAOIs (monoamine oxidase inhibitors) cannot be taken together. This combination can lead to serious and possibly even fatal reactions.

If I have other emotional problems in addition to OCD, will they also be treated with drugs?

Not necessarily. Certain personality disorders and problems such as low self-esteem benefit more from psychotherapy than medication.

Are there any medications I should avoid while taking an antiobsessive medication?

An SSRI should never be taken with a MAOI (monoamine oxidase inhibitor), as this combination can lead to serious and possibly even fatal reactions. Discuss other potential interactions with your physician, and always tell your doctor about all other medications (whether prescription or over-the-counter) and alternative remedies you are taking.

Can I safely drink alcohol or smoke marijuana while taking an antiobsessive medication?

No. Alcohol and marijuana can undermine the positive effects of drug therapy. Alcohol is a depressant and can aggravate your symptoms. Marijuana should be strictly avoided. In addition to the fact that it is illegal, it interferes with the action of neurotransmitters.

Can I take an antiobsessive medication safely during pregnancy? Will it harm my unborn child?

The ideal is not to be on any medication whatsoever when you are pregnant. Every food you eat and drug you take is passed on to your developing fetus through the placenta. While research in animals does not show that medications for OCD cause birth defects, animal studies are not always a certain indicator of how a drug will affect human beings. But if your OCD is so severe and disabling that it may have detrimental effects on the fetus, and the symptoms cannot be controlled with behavior therapy alone, your doctor may recommend that you continue taking medication.

Is it safe to take an antiobsessive medication while breastfeeding?

As during pregnancy, it's best to avoid all medications when breastfeeding, since everything you ingest is passed on to your growing baby via your breast milk. If your obsessive-compulsive symptoms are so severe and disabling that you require medication, you should discuss with your doctor whether it is safe to continue breastfeeding or whether you should switch your baby to formula.

Are antiobsessive medications safe enough for children to take?

Yes, but drug therapy should be closely monitored by a child psychiatrist.

Will taking an antiobsessive drug for a long period cause any long-term damage?

Not that we know of. Both clomipramine and the SSRIs have been used for a number of years without causing any irreversible difficulties. But keep in mind that drugs like Prozac have been around only since 1988. While they seem relatively safe, only time will tell for certain.

Do I have to take any medical tests prior to treatment with an antiobsessive medication?

Yes. Your doctor may order a number of tests to rule out other conditions that may be causing OCD and to make sure that you are well enough to withstand the side effects of medication. The tests generally include:

- A complete blood count (CBC), to check for anemia
- A chem screen, to assess liver and kidney function and measure electrolytes (the levels of potassium, sodium, and calcium in your blood)
- A urinalysis, to assess kidney function
- A thyroid profile (especially the thyroid-stimulating hormone or TSH test), because thyroid abnormalities manifest themselves as anxiety and depression
- An electrocardiogram (EKG), because clomipramine (not SSRIs) can have effects on conduction in the heart, and it is necessary to have a baseline to go by

How often do I need to see my doctor when taking an antiobsessive medication?

Several appointments are usually necessary to establish a diagnosis and make decisions about treatment. If you are to have behavior therapy as well as medication, your appointments will probably be weekly. Otherwise you will be asked to come back within the month to see if the medication is taking effect and to talk about any adverse side effects. Once your symptoms have diminished and you are on a stable dose of medication, appointments are less frequent. Whenever you experience a severe or unexpected reaction to your medication, notify your doctor immediately.

How much do antiobsessive medications cost?

The cost depends on a number of factors, including your dosage, the area of the country you live in, and the pharmacy you use. In addition, some health plans cover prescriptions and others don't. Generally speaking, the monthly costs for SSRIs range between $50 and $250. In contrast, a generic version of clomipramine—which has been on the market for a longer period of time—might cost as little as ten dollars a month.

My health care plan doesn't cover prescription drugs. Is there any other way of cutting my costs?

When cost is an issue, by all means be frank and open about this with your therapist. She may be able to help by giving you free samples left by drug company representatives. Alternatively, most drug companies provide a limited amount of antidepressants to people who cannot otherwise afford them. Your therapist can tell you how to take advantage of these programs.

Using generic drugs is another way to cut costs. Whether a drug is available generically depends on how long it has been on the market. This means that there are not yet generic versions of SSRIs, which are relatively new. But the tricyclic antidepressant clomipramine has been around for some time and is obtainable generically.

Will my health plan cover visits to my therapist to obtain new prescriptions?

As in the case of behavior therapy, coverage depends on the type of insurance you have and your diagnosis. Most health plans make a distinction between physical illness and mental illness. This completely overlooks the fact that many mental illnesses—including OCD—do have biological causes or underpinnings. Nevertheless the majority of plans limit the number of mental health visits you are allowed in a year; have a larger copayment for them; and place a lifetime cap on how much they will pay for mental health visits.

I've reached my health plan's limit for mental health visits. What should I do?

Obsessive-compulsive disorder is a serious condition, and one thing you should *not* do is ignore it. It may be that you will have to pay for your treatment out of your own pocket. If this is a hardship, ask your therapist whether she offers a sliding scale (a discount for those who cannot pay the full fee).

When antiobsessive medication and behavior therapy fail to control severe OCD, what happens next? Is hospitalization necessary?

Unlike in other psychiatric problems such as depression, hospitalization for OCD is uncommon. It is restricted to very severe cases when nothing else works. If OCD becomes so disabling that your level of living is compromised, hospitalization is an option. If your anxiety is overwhelming, and your obsessions and compulsions have spiraled out of control, interfering with your ability to function, a hospital may be the best place for you to be. This is essential in cases where the OCD sufferer becomes suicidal due to major depression caused by OCD.

What can I expect to happen at a hospital?

When OCD is this severe, a hospital may be the best environment in which to safely determine the best possible drug (or combination of drugs) at the lowest effective dose to diminish anxiety and begin to manage obsessions and compulsions. Once your symptoms are under some degree of control, a hospital provides a safe haven in which you can learn valuable techniques to control disturbing thoughts and intrusive rituals. Very intensive behavior therapy can take place, often with the aid of family involvement. In very troubled times the controlled environment of a hospital setting can provide a necessary respite from anxiety and pressures, helping you navigate your way through especially intense and disruptive symptoms.

Is surgery ever necessary for OCD?

Surgery for OCD is rare. But occasionally symptoms become overwhelming, completely interfering with your ability to live a normal life. When all else fails, your doctor may recommend neurosurgery to control OCD. Surgery involves disconnecting the outflow pathways from the orbitofrontal cortex.

Chapter 8

ALTERNATIVE THERAPIES FOR OCD

Aside from medication and therapy, what other treatments are available to help people who have obsessive-compulsive disorder?

While most people who have OCD can benefit from medication, behavior therapy, or both, rarely do the symptoms completely disappear. This leads many OCD sufferers to seek out alternative remedies for their disease. Alternatives include anything from herbal remedies to yoga to meditation to changes in diet.

Do alternative therapies really help?

There is little or no evidence to suggest that alternative therapies specifically work for OCD, but with the approval of your doctor you may try them in addition to medication and/or behavior therapy. If an alternative treatment helps you manage your stress, then it may help prevent OCD symptoms.

Are alternative treatments ever harmful?

It's possible. For example, herbal remedies have exploded in popularity in the 1990s. Yet just because they are natural substances does not mean that herbs are inherently safe. Like regular medications, herbs can enhance your health—but they are potent substances, and safety precautions should be carefully exercised when using them.

Should I consult with my doctor before trying an alternative therapy?

In most cases, yes. If you want to try a little yoga or meditation, go ahead. But before you try an herb or 5-hydroxy-tryptophan, be sure to consult with your doctor or therapist. Potential side effects and interactions must be carefully taken into account.

What about diet, exercise, and other lifestyle considerations? Can they affect OCD?

Of course. The stronger you are in body and mind, the more likely you are to be able to control day-to-day stress and deal with periodic crises. Being strong and healthy can't cure your OCD, but it can go a long way to helping you keep stress—a major trigger of OCD symptoms—under control.

LIFESTYLE CHANGES

Can changes in my lifestyle really improve my overall health?

Absolutely. A healthy lifestyle—especially getting a proper balance of rest and exercise, learning stress management techniques, following a healthy diet, maintaining a normal weight, avoiding bad habits, and taking a regular vitamin and mineral supplement—is your best protection against diseases of all kinds.

What constitutes a healthy diet?

A well-balanced diet emphasizes whole grains, fresh fruits and vegetables, legumes, nuts, seeds, and fish. Avoid caffeine-packed coffee, tea, and colas, which can be overly stimulating. If you are taking medication for OCD, drink no alcohol at all. Otherwise limit your alcohol consumption to one drink a day. Eliminate or cut back on refined sugar. Among other things, this means no more cookies, cake, and sugary cereals. Sugar provides an initial burst of energy but is soon followed by a crash. Virtually everyone can benefit from a high-potency vitamin and mineral supplement.

I feel worn out all the time, which makes me feel more fragile and vulnerable to stress. Can improvements in my diet increase my energy level?

Yes. A balanced diet and regular exercise can boost your energy. If this doesn't help, get a regular medical evaluation to determine if you have medical problems such as anemia or thyroid irregularities.

EXERCISE YOUR BODY

Can exercise help control emotional problems?

Exercise can provide a general sense of well-being, reduce stress, and help you get a good night's sleep. All kinds of exercises are good for you. Stretches are calming and soothing, especially when they are done in combination with deep breathing. Regular aerobic exercises such as walking, swimming, bicycling, golfing, and playing ball are among the many enjoyable ways to keep blood flowing around your body, including to your brain. A 1995 study found that five thousand college students reduced anxiety and depression through regular exercise.

Is yoga helpful?

Yoga is an approach to emotional and physical wellness that combines exercise, breathing, and meditation. The slow and deliberate postures of yoga, with their careful attention to controlled breathing, help control stress and anxiety. If you practice even as few as three yoga exercises for as little as twenty minutes a day, you'll soon feel more relaxed.

What is an example of a relaxing yoga position?

The yoga position known as the Tree is a good stretch to calm your mind. Since this posture calls for balance and concentration, it helps you block out mental distractions and focuses your attention on your body. This creates a relaxation response, relieving anxiety and enabling you to proceed with your day in a more relaxed, focused, and productive frame of mind.

To do the Tree, stand and focus on one spot at eye level in the wall in front of you. Slowly raise your right foot and place it on the inside of your left thigh. Place the palms of your hands together in front of your chest. When you get your balance, breathe in, and slowly raise your arms (with your palms still joined) over your head. Hold for a count of three. Lean one hand against a wall or chair if you have difficulty balancing. Repeat with your left foot.

Is rest important too?

Absolutely. In our busy society, we often don't get enough sleep. To boost energy and alertness, try to fill in your sleep gaps with a twenty-to-thirty minute catnap in the afternoon. Longer naps can leave you feeling groggy instead of energized. (For specific tips on how to get a good night's sleep, turn to Chapter 9.)

What about a massage?

Anything that relaxes you is a good idea, and massage can have a very calming effect on the nervous system. Licensed massage therapists use a combination of motions such as kneading, chopping, and applied pressure to relax and ease tension in your muscles. As in acupuncture, the motions of massage are thought to at least temporarily interfere with the peripheral nervous system, providing relief as they prevent pain signals from being sent to the brain.

RELAX YOUR MIND

What mind-body techniques can I use to relax and control the level of stress in my life?

Meditation, deep breathing, and visualization are just a few of many, many helpful stress-management techniques. The ability to relax and get a handle on stress is crucial to the success of any program to relieve anxiety disorders like OCD. Mind-body techniques are designed to help you achieve a state of deep relaxation.

What is deep relaxation?

Deep relaxation means more than slumping on the couch at the end of the day and turning on the TV. The deep relaxation that comes with meditation and yoga brings forth a number of physiological and psychological responses. These include:

- Decreases in heart rate, respiration rate, blood pressure, muscle tension, and metabolic rate
- Decrease in general anxiety level
- A break in the cumulative effects of stress

- Increased energy level, productivity, concentration, and memory

Is meditation helpful for people with OCD?

Meditation can be a helpful auxiliary strategy for managing OCD. Meditation will not cure OCD (remember that nothing can), but it can help control your symptoms by reducing your stress-hormone level, heart rate, and blood pressure. Many people begin to meditate for only five minutes at a time and find it so satisfying that they gradually extend their sessions.

What is the goal of meditation?

People who meditate achieve deep mental and physical relaxation while remaining awake and alert. Meditation helps you reach a state of inner and outer peace.

What is the cost of meditation?

Meditation is free. Moreover, it doesn't involve any drugs, and almost anyone can learn to do it.

Are there different kinds of meditation?

Yes. Three of the most popular forms are transcendental meditation, the relaxation response, and progressive relaxation.

What is transcendental meditation?

This type of meditation involves sitting quietly for about twenty minutes while your mind focuses on a sound, or mantra, while you breathe deeply. Concentration on a single mantra such as *om* rids your mind of day-to-day concerns and helps you focus and relax. Another form of meditation is to direct your attention to a sensory memory, such as the heat of the sun on your body as you listen to ocean waves rolling into shore.

What is the relaxation response?

This is a similar technique created by Harvard cardiologist Dr. Herbert Benson, in which people choose a soothing word to focus on twice a day.

What is progressive relaxation?

Although there are many different types of progressive relaxation, try beginning with this simple exercise. Dim the lights, and turn the answering machine down to make sure you're not disturbed. Close your eyes and relax. Search within yourself for any tension, and release it. Breathing in, visualize the muscles of the body, starting with your face. Breathing out, relax the face muscles. Gradually move downward, to the neck and shoulders, the spine, the arms, the torso, the legs, consciously relaxing every muscle in your body.

What about breathing exercises? Can they help me relax?

Studies have found differences in the breathing of people who are relaxed and those who are anxious. When you are fearful or shaking a stranger's hand or walking out of your house, you may notice that your breaths are more rapid and shallow. In contrast, deep breathing has a naturally calming effect on the sympathetic nervous system.

Choose a quiet time and place, and try this exercise. Slowly take a deep breath in, hold for a count of three, and exhale. Then simply sit quietly, resting one hand on your stomach, and feel your breath pass in and out of your body. Watch yourself breathe for the balance of the minute. If your mind starts to wander, gently draw it back. Just be aware of your breath: in and out. This is mindful breathing.

What is biofeedback?

Biofeedback is yet another way to control stress. In this technique small electrodes are placed on your forehead, and electronic sensors are then used to measure your body's automatic functions, such as muscles that contract due to tension, breathing patterns, and pulse rate. As you practice different relaxation methods (for example, meditation), feedback from the sensors shows whether you are successfully relaxing your muscles and slowing your pulse. The goal is to teach you to consciously relax your own muscles, by watching and reducing the level of electrical responses on the gauge reading.

What about aromatherapy?

Aromatherapy is the art of using essential oils distilled from plants, flowers, fruits, and trees to enhance your well-being. Many essential oils have a calming and tranquilizing effect, inducing a general sense of well-being and relieving the restless and agitated mind. Try a soothing lavender or vanilla bath, or a full-body massage with clary sage, orange, rose, sandalwood, frankincense, or ylang-ylang.

HERBAL THERAPY

What is herbal therapy?

Herbal therapy is the use of remedies prepared from roots, leaves, and other parts of plants for healing purposes. It is a holistic approach that emphasizes promoting health and preventing disease. Along with other alternative therapies, herbalism has become very popular as more and more people make the connection between body and mind, in this case stress and a greater risk of disease.

According to herbal theory, specific ailments are the eventual outcome of both lifestyle choices and genetic predisposition. This means that even though you can't change the fact that a problem like OCD runs in your family, you can take steps to prevent it through control of stress and anxiety. Herbal remedies, natural stress-management techniques, a healthy diet, and a proper balance of rest and exercise are thought to be the keys to coping with stress and anxiety.

Are herbal remedies safe?

Many important questions about herbal safety have yet to be answered. In this country herbal remedies are sold not as drugs but as dietary supplements. As a result, they do not have to be tested and approved by the FDA. In fact, they are not tested, approved, or inspected by any federal agency. Scientific trials of herbs have mostly taken place abroad, especially in Germany, where herbs are prescribed by doctors just like conventional medicines.

I'm on an antiobsessive medication. Should I be concerned about possible interactions?

Absolutely. Do not combine St. John's wort with antidepressants or kava with benzodiazepines, since these drugs and herbs have similar actions in your body. Ginkgo should not be taken with any blood thinners, including aspirin. There are many other possible interactions and side effects of herbs, which is why it is essential to speak to your doctor before using a plant remedy.

Are there any general safety precautions that should be followed when using herbs?

Modern research confirms that herbs have a significant impact on the body, and plant remedies must be treated with the respect due to any medicinal substance. If you decide to give herbal remedies a try, here are a few basic safety guidelines to follow:

- Always consult with your doctor or therapist before taking any herbal remedy. While herbal remedies may complement medical care of a serious health problem such as OCD, they are not meant to replace it.
- If you are taking an SSRI or other medication, check with your doctor and pharmacist about possibly harmful interactions.
- Begin with the lowest recommended dosage of an herb, and increase gradually as needed.
- Do not exceed the recommended dosages. Just because an herb (or drug) works well at one particular dose does not mean that it works better in larger amounts.
- If you are over sixty-five or suffer from compromised liver or kidney function, reduce the recommended dosages by 30 percent.
- If you are pregnant or nursing, do not use herbal remedies.
- Stop taking an herb if you experience any adverse reaction, such as nausea, vomiting, diarrhea, or an allergic reaction. If your reaction is severe, go to the emergency room of the nearest hospital.
- Always purchase herbs and herbal remedies from the most reputable sources you can find.

The herbal antidepressant St. John's wort has received a lot of press in the last year or two. Can it help control the symptoms of OCD?

St. John's wort may be helpful if you're depressed, but it's unclear whether it has any impact on OCD. This herb has long been a valued remedy for depression in Europe, where studies have found it to be as effective as tricyclic antidepressants in treating mild to moderate (not severe) depression. To avoid overmedication, St. John's wort should never be combined with any prescription antidepressants. Occasional side effects include mild nausea, lack of appetite, and fatigue. One study indicated that large dosages may cause increased sensitivity to the sun.

Kava has also received a great deal of media attention. Can it really help control anxiety?

Americans spent $15 million on kava in 1996, and twice that amount in 1997, according to the *Nutrition Business Journal*. German studies have suggested that kava can relieve emotional trauma and sleep disturbances. Yet although kava may seem like an attractive alternative to those who suffer from stress and anxiety, new studies point to potential problems with this herb.

Can any herbal remedies help with the sexual side effects of antiobsession medications?

Ginkgo biloba may be useful in treating the sexual side effects of SSRIs such as Prozac. Extracted from the fan-shaped leaves of one of the world's most ancient trees, more than 10 million ginkgo prescriptions are written by German and French physicians each year, making it the most commonly prescribed herbal medicine in the world. An invaluable antioxidant, ginkgo stimulates blood flow and oxygen supply to the brain and heart, in fact all around the body. Ginkgo may remedy male impotence by increasing penile blood flow.

AMINO ACIDS

What do amino acids have to do with OCD?

As you learned in Chapter 4, obsessive-compulsive symptoms are brought about by an imbalance of serotonin levels in the brain. Amino acids are precursors of serotonin, dopamine, and other neurotransmitters. This means that they are the raw materials, or building blocks of protein, from which mood-regulating chemicals like serotonin are made. One alternative approach to treating OCD is to increase your consumption of amino acids.

Which amino acid is linked to OCD?

Tryptophan is the specific precursor that your body converts first into 5-hydroxy-tryptophan and then into serotonin.

Has any research been done on whether tryptophan really helps?

Some doctors have met with success in prescribing this amino acid, a precursor of serotonin, along with clomipramine. Since amino acids form neurotransmitters in the body, an imbalance in amino acids could theoretically lead to an imbalance in neurotransmitters. No controlled studies, however, have confirmed that it helps, and oral tryptophan is currently unavailable in this country. This is because of a contamination incident in 1989, in which tryptophan produced by one manufacturer caused an illness called eosinophilia-myalgia syndrome (a condition of severe muscle and joint pain, weakness, swelling, and shortness of breath). It is possible that oral tryptophan will become available again. In the meantime a possible alternative is 5-hydroxy-tryptophan, which is available by prescription from compounding pharmacies.

What are some natural sources of tryptophan?

Tryptophan-rich foods include dairy products, turkey, nuts, and bananas. It turns out that your grandmother was right about drinking a relaxing glass of warm milk before going to bed. Good dairy sources of tryptophan include low-fat milk, ice milk, yogurt, hard cheeses, and cottage cheese.

Chapter 9

PREVENTION OF OCD

Can obsessive thoughts and compulsive rituals be prevented?

Not with absolute certainty. As you know by now, once you have OCD, you have it for life. There is no cure. But there are many steps that you can take to prevent symptoms from recurring.

What can I do to minimize my risk of future recurrences of OCD?

Although there is no surefire way to prevent obsessions and compulsions, following these steps is your best bet:

- Work with your therapist to find the treatment that works for you, and stick with it.

- Take your medication as prescribed. Do not skip doses. Never stop or change your dosage without consulting your doctor.

- Practice exposure-and-response prevention homework by yourself, with a helper, or with your therapist.

- Involve your family in your treatment.

- Monitor your lifestyle, and take good care of yourself.

What are the risk factors for future recurrences of OCD?

The symptoms of OCD wax and wane over the years, and many times there is no way to know that a recurrence is about to take place. We do know, however, that stressful experiences or the negative impact of cumulative stress can bring on the symptoms of OCD.

If you're about to make a major transition—for instance, if you're planning to move or change jobs or get divorced—it's good to be aware that it may spark a return of OCD symptoms. If you've been under a lot of pressure at work or are experiencing marital difficulties, the effects of cumulative stress can wear you down and lower your resistance to any number of health problems. In this case you should also be wary of the signs of OCD, such as more frequent showering or checking. (Turn to Chapter 4 to learn more about stress and its role in OCD.)

When I know I'm going to be faced with a stressful situation, what can I do in advance to prevent it from triggering OCD?

See your therapist and discuss going back on medication for a time, and revisit your behavior therapy more actively. Also pay attention to your lifestyle.

If you allow stress to make you overtired and irritable, you may be more likely to have a relapse.

Can medication and behavior therapy prevent obsessive-compulsive symptoms from developing again?

Not with 100 percent certainty, but this is your best bet to prevent symptoms from recurring.

Will the same symptoms that brought on my first experience with OCD signal that I am about to have a recurrence?

Probably not. Obsessive-compulsive symptoms come in all different shapes and sizes, waxing and waning in both their variety and their intensity over time. In some cases OCD lies dormant for years following a childhood problem, only to emerge again at full force in your twenties when you get married or change jobs. Your symptoms as an adult may be very different from those you experienced as a child. When you were nine or ten, you might have washed your hands again and again due to a fear of dirt and germs. As an adult, your OCD might manifest itself in unreasonable anxiety about the health of a loved one or an excessive need for symmetry and order in your home.

I'm happy about the changes in my life. Why should they cause OCD symptoms?

Even if you are very happy about your marriage or new career, major changes in your life are always challenging and emotionally traumatic. Whether stress is brought on by a cheerful event or a sorrowful transition, it can trigger the symptoms of OCD.

If I notice warning signs of a recurrence, how long should I wait before contacting my therapist?

Consult with your therapist as soon as you notice any ominous signs, such as more frequent hand-washing or checking or an increase in anxiety and uncomfortable, unwelcome thoughts. It's best to address obsessive thoughts and rituals before they become thoroughly entrenched. Your therapist can help you decide what is best to do next. She may ask you to come in for a booster session of exposure-and-response prevention or suggest that you go back on medication for a time.

What kinds of situations can trigger OCD?

It's important to identify the stressful situations that you may face in your life. They may include:

- Death of a family member or close friend
- Marriage or divorce
- A move
- Getting fired or changing jobs
- Holidays
- Anniversaries of sad events

How does stress affect my health?

Chronic stress sets into motion a cascade of events involving serotonin as well as dozens of other chemicals in your body. This kind of stress weakens your immune system and lowers your resistance to disease. Wounds heal more slowly, latent viruses like herpes are more likely to erupt, and brain cells are affected. Although we don't know exactly how this happens, it's clear that OCD symptoms too may be triggered by stress.

Can reducing stress really prevent the emergence of obsessive-compulsive symptoms?

In many cases, yes. When you are strong and healthy and feel like you have your life under control, your body is better able to resist diseases of all kinds.

What are examples of strategies that I can use to manage stress?

There are many, many strategies to beat stress. Simple things such as exercise, taking a bath, reading a book, and talking to a friend can help release tension. Or you might try more formal relaxation strategies such as meditation, visualization, and biofeedback. To derive the most benefits from these techniques, give them time. (For more information on alternative therapies like these, turn to Chapter 8. To learn about an even wider variety of coping strategies for OCD, see Chapter 10.)

Is there anything else I can or should do to prevent obsessive-compulsive symptoms?

Behavior therapy and medication are the best weapons against recurrences of OCD. But it's also important to pay attention to your overall health. Try to stay strong in both body and mind. When you eat right, get a good balance of exercise and rest, and practice good stress management, you're arming yourself well against a variety of health problems.

Can a healthy diet prevent OCD?

No. But it can play a key role in maintaining your overall health, which in turn can help you cope with stressful situations in a more productive manner. A healthy diet is now considered a major protection against a wide range of diseases. Try to limit your intake of refined carbohydrates, alcohol, and coffee.

Can exercise prevent OCD?

Again the answer is no. It would be difficult, however, to overstate the many health benefits of exercise. In addition to reducing your risk of heart disease, high blood pressure, and some cancers, exercise can calm your mind. Even moderate exercise such as walking or gardening stimulates the release of feel-good chemicals called endorphins in your brain. (Read more about exercise in Chapter 8.)

Planning my wedding is making me toss and turn all night. Can getting a good night's sleep help me control stress and keep my OCD at bay?

Getting restorative sleep is essential when you're under stress. A number of natural strategies can help you sleep more contentedly:

• Use your bed only for sleeping and making love. Your bed is not made for other activities, such as watching TV or working on your laptop. If you're restless and can't get to sleep, go into the living room and watch TV or read a book for half an hour. Then return to your bed and try again to go to sleep.

• Be sure you have a comfortable bed and a supportive pillow.

• Keep your bedroom completely dark and as free of noise as possible. Use a white noise generator, a water fountain, or tapes of nature, ocean, or rain sounds to block out noise. Or invest in earplugs.

• Choose lightweight quilts to keep heavy, uncomfortable covers off your feet.

• Go to bed at night and get up in the morning at the same times, in order to assist your body in establishing normal rhythms.

• In the hour before you go to sleep, avoid stimulants such as the TV, computer, and bright lights.

Can working at behavior therapy with a friend help prevent OCD? Is asking a family member or friend to participate in my treatment helpful?

Yes, and yes again. It's vital that you not allow yourself to become isolated from your loved ones. This can lead to depression and other emotional problems. Even more important, a close friend or family member can practice exposure-and-response prevention with you and encourage you to resist your urges.

How do I choose the right person to help me with behavior therapy?

Select a family member or close friend with whom you can openly and honestly share your experiences of OCD and your treatment goals. This should be a strong person who will not stand idle while you simply give in to urges or replace one ritual with another. It's also helpful to pick someone who is not judgmental. You want to feel free to ask "silly" questions, for you may no longer be able to distinguish between what's reasonable and what's not. If you're not sure whether it is appropriate to double-check your papers or your housework or your locks, you should feel comfortable asking your helper.

Can my helper reassure me that it's not necessary to perform a ritual?

No. It's not your helper's role to reassure you again and again that all's well, relieving your anxiety and therefore your need to perform a ritual. Difficult as it may be, the goal of behavior therapy is to eventually enable you to make these kinds of decisions yourself. You should feel free, however, to ask your helper questions about what constitutes normal behavior.

If my helper can't reassure me, exactly what is his or her role in my behavior therapy?

A helper can do you the most good by following these guidelines:

- Don't offer reassurances, but do answer questions about what is appropriate or safe and what's not.
- Don't answer these questions more than once. Gently but firmly tell the OCD sufferer that she already knows the answer to that question.
- Encourage her to resist the tug of obsessions and compulsions.
- Don't be overly critical.
- Be patient.
- Praise every small achievement.
- Approach problems with wit and humor, but without making fun of symptoms.
- Don't allow yourself to be drawn into arguments during exposure-and-response prevention sessions.

Is it true that my disease affects my whole family?

OCD affects every aspect of your life: your family, your friends, and your relationships at work. Strained relationships and social isolation are typical consequences of this difficult disease. After all, it's very trying to live with an exacting perfectionist or someone whose painful doubts require constant reassurances. Love and marriage are especially difficult for people who suffer from OCD, who think and do things that seem to make no sense and then try to hide this from loved ones. Anger and resentment are often the end result of poor communication between you and other family members and a lack of understanding about your disease.

My family thinks I should just get over my OCD and move on with my life. Are they right?

No. Many people mistakenly think that OCD sufferers should "just get over it." But OCD is a disease that requires treatment with either medication or behavior therapy or both. Your family needs to learn that controlling your obsessions and compulsions is not just a matter of exercising your willpower.

My husband tells me I am selfish and should think of someone besides myself for a change. But how can I, when all my time is taken up dealing with my disease?

People with OCD are typically very self-absorbed. When demanding thoughts and rituals command the majority of your attention and time, it is very hard to see a situation from another person's point of view. Your focus is on meeting your own needs, not on satisfying anyone else's.

Self-absorption is a symptom of your disease, however, and not a personality trait. It may be very helpful for your husband to understand this distinction. With proper treatment you can control your symptoms and devote more time and attention to your relationship with your husband.

I feel such anger at my family and sometimes lose my temper at them for no reason at all. What can I do about this?

As your symptoms improve with treatment, you will find that your anger recedes as well. Your fears and rituals are so frustrating for both you and your family that it's no wonder there is a lot of anger and hostility. When you're receiving regular medical treatment, you'll feel calmer.

What happens if I don't get treatment for my OCD?

In very severe cases an all-engrossing immersion in obsessions and rituals comes to take up the entire day, gradually destroying normal family lives and wrecking careers and friendships. It may get to the point where it takes three hours to get dressed in the morning and another three to reverse the process at night. You may grow paralyzed with fears of germs and disease and eventually become unable to leave the house to enter the "contaminated" world outside. You may have to check again and again with a parent or spouse—sometimes hundreds of times—for reassurance that you have not accidentally harmed them and that they are not mad at you. This is exasperating for everyone concerned and can lead to the disintegration of families.

We've painted a pretty bleak picture here, but without appropriate treatment it can—and does—happen. In extreme cases obsessive thoughts and rituals are so demanding and time-consuming that they leave time for neither a job nor any sort of personal life. Fortunately, however, today very effective treatments with drugs and behavior therapy can prevent these kinds of calamities from occurring.

Should I tell my friends about my OCD?

It is a good idea—although do distinguish between your close friends and your casual acquaintances. There's no need for everyone in your office or at the gym to know about your disease. But with close friends you have no reason to be ashamed of the symptoms of your OCD. After all, OCD is an illness, just like heart disease or diabetes.

Hiding obsessions and compulsions can also cause more problems than being open and honest about them. Symptoms such as fears of contamination or checking behavior will otherwise strike people as odd or excessive. Although it can be difficult to tell a friend or especially someone you're dating about your illness, if the friendship or relationship is strong enough, they will understand and distinguish between you and your illness. Remember: You are not your illness.

What can my family and friends do to help me prevent OCD?

Fortunately there are many positive actions that your family and friends can take to help you deal with your disease. They include:

- Do everything you can to help your loved one stop performing rituals.
- Do not perform his rituals for him.
- Do not help him or enable him to carry out his rituals.
- If his fears are irrational, do not agree with them.
- Gently refuse to answer obsessional questions over and over.
- Don't try to convince an OCD sufferer that his fears and obsessions are false or inaccurate.
- Walk away when you are frustrated or angry or losing your patience.
- Never make an OCD sufferer feel that his thoughts and rituals are crazy or unsafe.
- Applaud him for small improvements.
- Be encouraging. When he feels that his situation is hopeless, point out how far he's come already.
- Try to help the OCD sufferer control guilt, frustration, and anger. Stressful emotional traumas

like these can trigger OCD symptoms or make them worse.

- Use wit and humor to defuse tense situations, but beware of saying anything that might be considered making fun of OCD.

- Avoid making any comparisons to his behavior prior to developing OCD. You can, however, make positive comments about how much he has improved since starting treatment.

What is the most important thing for my family to learn about OCD?

Perhaps the most vital lesson for your family to learn is that OCD is a biochemically driven disease. Your obsessions and compulsions, which cause you great pain, are not something you are doing to drive your family crazy. You are not weak. You are not lazy. You cannot "just stop" experiencing symptoms. While these realizations may not make your symptoms any less frustrating or disruptive to family members, more compassion and less anger usually come about with a greater understanding of OCD. Interestingly, sometimes when you tell people to whom you're biologically related about your problem, they may become aware that issues that they're struggling with are also symptomatic of OCD.

What are some of the mistakes families make when contending with obsessions and compulsions?

Out of the very best of intentions, families often do all the wrong things when struggling to handle the problems of OCD. Very often the whole family is drawn into the web of this disease, leading increasingly unorthodox lives in order to accommodate the mother or brother or son who suffers from OCD. In order to avoid conflict and dissension, family members may perform the rituals for the OCD sufferer themselves, or take steps to make it easier for him to engage in them. Some try to get the person with OCD to just stop performing rituals. Once your family learns that these kinds of actions are making things worse and not better, they can help you deal more effectively with OCD.

Is it helpful if my family members perform my rituals for me?

No. Out of the very best of impulses, your family members may try to defuse a difficult situation by performing your rituals for you. For example, to keep you from anxiously checking and rechecking that the doors and windows are locked at night, your wife might do it for you. Or perhaps it is your spouse who harbors contamination fears. In consequence, as soon as you come home from work every day, you strip your clothes off and throw them into the washing machine, setting the dial for very hot water and adding industrial-strength detergent. Then you jump into the shower to remove the dirt and germs from the outside world.

But this is no way to live—you are simply helping a family member give in to OCD fears and urges by performing rituals for her or him. If the OCD sufferer does not resist these compelling urges and impulses for himself or herself, they will not diminish in intensity.

What about family members who make it easier for OCD sufferers to perform rituals?

This is another way in which family members inadvertently support OCD. For example, it may be easier for your mother to give in to your contamination fears and buy extra soap at the supermarket for you each week and quietly stow it away under the bathroom sink. But in the long run, enabling you to engage in ritualistic behavior is the easy way out and does nothing to dull the long-term impact of your obsessions and compulsions.

What about family members who try to stop me from performing rituals? Are they helping?

No. If you have a child who must tug on her hair, circle the dining-room table three times, and touch a certain bear or bunny before agreeing to go to school every morning, your temptation may very well be to tell her to just stop it. If you're leaving on vacation and your spouse runs back into the house to check that the gas on the stove is off for a third, fourth, and fifth time, you may scream at him to just get over it and get in the car. As you probably have reason to know already, this doesn't work. For your entire week in Aruba, while you're sunbathing on the beach, your husband will probably be worrying about having accidentally caused the house to burn down. You cannot simply stop OCD behavior. OCD requires medical treatment.

How can I learn more about preventing OCD?

The Obsessive-Compulsive Foundation in Milford, Connecticut, is one of the best sources of information about OCD. Turn to Appendix A for the addresses and phone numbers of this and other helpful professional associations. In Appendix B you will find many books that can help you discover even more information about obsessive-compulsive disorder. The more you learn about OCD, the better you will be able to cope with your disease and prevent painful recurrences.

Chapter 10

COPING WITH OBSESSIVE-COMPULSIVE DISORDER

Since medication and behavior therapy can often control obsessions and compulsions, why do I need to bother with coping skills?

There are several reasons. When you experience obsessions and compulsions, medications and behavior therapy are very effective treatments. Yet both can take time. It may be four to six weeks before an antiobsessive medication has any impact on your symptoms and up to three months before it takes full effect. If one drug doesn't work, then your doctor will switch medications.

Behavior therapy is also a gradual process, requiring an average of ten to twelve weeks and sometimes even longer. Fortunately, once you've mastered the skills of exposure-and-response prevention, they can last you a lifetime. When stress leads to a recurrence of OCD symptoms, your best bet is to schedule a booster session or two of behavior therapy with a mental health professional to brush up on your skills.

Many of the coping strategies we discuss in this chapter are a direct outgrowth of behavior therapy. Over the years you'll probably find that you evolve into your own best behavior therapist. It's you who monitor your own behavior and are alert to the signs of obsessive-compulsive behavior. If you find yourself showering or washing your hands more often than usual, it's time to take action. There are many positive steps you can take every day to control intrusive thoughts and habits.

What can I do to cope with obsessive and compulsive symptoms?

Experts suggest that a two-pronged approach to OCD is best. Stress is a trigger of OCD, and it's therefore important to control your exposure to cumulative stress and anxiety. But this does not mean that you should avoid the triggers of your OCD symptoms.

The coping skills you learn in behavior therapy can help you resist the tyranny of obsessions and compulsions. As we saw in Chapter 6, the key is to confront situations that make you anxious and then deliberately ignore the accompanying urges to perform anxiety-releasing rituals. When you see that nothing bad happens in consequence, it will loosen the hold that your disease has on you. You'll feel better. It is counterproductive to avoid every single situation that makes you anxious. When you give in and perform rituals to feel relief that moment, you deepen the hold that OCD has on you, making matters progressively worse in the long run.

Try to strike a balance, trimming excess stress from your lifestyle but refusing to avoid the situations that trigger your OCD. In this chapter you will find many tips and strategies that have helped other people cope with OCD through the years.

Do coping strategies really work?

For the majority of people who have OCD, yes. When you feel the pull of cleaning or checking or other kinds of urges, it's very helpful to be armed in advance with strategies to confront and defeat them. Mastering some of the coping mechanisms outlined in this chapter can give you control over the obsessions and compulsions of your disease. Many of these skills can also help you cope with the stressful situations that trigger OCD and the depression commonly experienced as a result of OCD. Good coping strategies can help you maintain your relationships with your family, friends, and coworkers.

COPING STRATEGIES

• If you're taking medication for OCD, don't skip a dose. Even if you feel better, a steady amount of medication must remain in your bloodstream in order to control OCD symptoms. If you stop taking antiobsessive medication before the agreed-upon time, you might experience a serious relapse.

• Keep all your appointments with your therapist. Even though behavior therapy may make you feel anxious at first, it will help you learn coping skills that will serve you over the course of your lifetime.

• Remind yourself every single day that OCD is a biochemical disease that is not your fault. There is no reason for you to feel guilty because you are ill.

• When obsessive thoughts prey upon you, confront them head-on. Nothing bad will happen if you don't wash your hands or check the appliances. If this is very difficult for you, ask a friend or family member to help. If necessary, schedule a booster session with your behavior therapist.

• Recognizing that anxiety is a normal reaction to exposure-and-response prevention, learn stress management techniques such as deep breathing, meditation, and visualization. (For detailed information on these techniques, turn to Chapter 8.)

• Don't be a perfectionist. When you have guests for dinner, the kitchen floor doesn't have to be clean enough to eat off and the books don't need to be in alphabetical order.

• Set realistic goals. Try not to expect too much of yourself. Give yourself a break.

• If you're uncomfortable entertaining friends when your home isn't immaculate and your cooking isn't up to gourmet standards, go the casual route instead and order in a pizza.

• Staying busy is an important way to control OCD behavior, but this doesn't mean that you have to become a martyr to your family or career. Try to avoid cumulative stress by learning to say no to one more ride to the mall or yet another project at work. Instead of always trying to live up to impossible standards of perfection, think of yourself for a change.

• Say no without making any excuses. Unless you're sharing personal concerns with a close friend or family member, your mental state is your business. You don't owe anyone else any explanations.

• Delegate whenever possible. At work, don't feel that you have to breathe down your secretary's neck. At home, encourage your child to be responsible for the state of her own homework, so that you don't have to review it every single night. If it's not perfect, recognize that that's okay. No disaster will result from your not checking everything yourself.

• Clear your schedule of unnecessary errands. Learn who delivers—restaurants, grocery stores, and pharmacies all do it. See how many other services you can find that arrive at your doorstep.

• Stay up-to-date with technology. Instead of hurrying off to the post office, e-mail your work in.

• Arrange for your phone and electric bills to be automatically paid from your checking account each month.

• Break each task into manageable parts. In that way it won't appear to be so overwhelming.

• Enlist a family member or close friend as a helper in your OCD recovery program. A friend can offer you feedback and support when your energy and efforts flag.

• Share your goals with your helper openly and honestly. Even if it seems embarrassing at first, it's an important way to follow through with your good intentions.

• When you're successful in meeting even a small short-term goal, reward yourself. Every little bit helps.

• Exercise to reduce general anxiety and also the stress brought on by warding off OCD symptoms. The relaxing postures of yoga or tai chi may prove especially beneficial. In addition, many researchers believe that aerobic exercise can naturally increase the chemical release of serotonin and lift your mood.

• After your workout, treat yourself to a relaxing visit to the sauna, steam room, or whirlpool. Have a massage.

• Get a proper balance of rest and exercise. If you're not getting enough sleep, you're opening the door to stress.

• Treat yourself to a day at the spa, and catch up on all the popular magazines you don't usually get a chance to read.

• Get your hair done, and at the same time have a manicure and pedicure.

• Relax your breathing. When you're experiencing anxious thoughts and feelings, you're not getting enough oxygen—or on the other hand you may be hyperventilating. Controlling your breathing is one of the age-old ways to relieve stress.

• Give yourself a pep talk. Replace the negativity of OCD with positive self-encouragements. Prepare a few phrases and repeat them to yourself several times a day. For example, say:

> "This is my OCD talking, not me."
>
> "I am not my illness."
>
> "I know it doesn't make sense to check this again."
>
> "I can handle this."
>
> "If I don't perform this ritual, nothing bad is going to happen to me or the people I love."
>
> "This will get easier."
>
> "Tomorrow is another day."
>
> "Nothing about these feelings is really dangerous. It just feels that way."
>
> "It's okay to make mistakes. No one's perfect."
>
> "I am not crazy, and resisting my urges will not drive me crazy."

> "I know that I will never act out an obsessional thought that will hurt someone."

• Write these statements on Post-its or index cards, and put them on your bathroom mirror or bulletin board. Tuck them in your briefcase or pocketbook.

• Eat a healthy diet. There is a definite link between diet and health.

• Since stress can deplete your supply of vitamins such as B6, take a regular vitamin and mineral supplement.

• Assiduously avoid false escape routes like alcohol and drugs. These are dangerous and addictive and will only worsen your problems.

• Do not suppress your feelings. If you are unhappy, indulge yourself with a good cry. If you are angry, it's okay to express this too. Locking in your anger is like letting acid eat away at your insides.

• Distinguish between genuine grief and biochemically caused anxiety and unhappiness. If a close friend or family member has died, of course you feel sad and lost in your bereavement. But if you feel that way for no concrete reason, it's important to realize this and take appropriate action.

• Spend time with friends and family who make you feel good.

• Call a friend. Schedule a date. Don't allow your obsessions and compulsions to isolate you from the rest of the world. Isolation leads to depression.

• Ask your friends over for a round of bridge or a board game.

• Get up out of bed and get dressed every morning, even if you don't have to and don't feel like it.

• If you find yourself huddled in the corner of an armchair at noon, still wearing your pajamas and waiting for the soaps to begin, call a friend instead and go out to lunch.

• Ask for help when you need it. In addition to family and friends, consult your rabbi, priest, or minister.

• If you're a student, contact a counselor at your school or college.

• Attend a service at your church or temple. Prayer can have a healing influence.

• Enroll in an adult education course. This is a good way to discover a new hobby or interest and to meet new people.

• Go to the pound and adopt a homeless cat or dog. Research shows that even petting an animal can lower your blood pressure and stress levels.

• Volunteer. Donating your time, energy and effort to others can be a deep source of satisfaction and take your mind off your symptoms.

• Even on a difficult day, try to have a gratitude moment. Is there anything you can think of that made you grateful today?

- Think positive. Don't let anyone else put you down—for anything.

- Make love with a trusted partner.

- Practice your favorite hobby. Whether that means knitting or painting or tossing a ball around with a friend, keeping busy in enjoyable ways is a good way to ward off OCD symptoms.

- Visit a favorite museum, or go to the ballet. Cultural experiences are both personally satisfying and an excellent way to meet like-minded people.

- Garden. Spending time outdoors in nature on a beautiful day can reduce your stress level and give you great satisfaction. If rows of vegetables aren't arranged with perfect symmetry, you will see that they can nonetheless thrive.

- Listen to music. If you're down in the dumps, put on some old Motown hits. If you're overwrought, unwind with some Beethoven or Brahms. Music stimulates the release of serotonin.

- Read a favorite book. Some people like to re-read all six Jane Austen novels every summer. It's like visiting an old friend, and discovering something new about them—and maybe about yourself too—every time.

- Join a reading group at your local bookstore. Even the large chains now recruit people to discuss books.

- Take in a movie.

- Spend time with your children, or ask a niece or nephew over for the day. Children are inspirational. They possess a disarming ability to relax and live in the moment.

• Take a cue from children, and live in the present. Don't brood about things that happened in the past, or worry too much about possible future disasters.

• Read a favorite volume of poetry, or compose your own haiku.

• Keep a journal. Often recording your feelings on paper makes you feel better, and later on you can review your writings to help you gain a deeper perspective. Many people with OCD keep track of each behavior therapy success in a journal. You too may find that this helps you come up with new solutions for old problems.

• Take a quiet walk in the woods or on the beach. Enjoy a beautiful sunset, and let go of your worries. Nature is a mighty serotonin booster.

• Learn more about OCD, its causes, and its treatment. Keep in mind that medication and behavior therapy can help control obsessive thoughts and compulsive rituals.

• Join a support group in your area for people who have OCD.

• Search the Internet for a chat room for people who are coping with OCD.

• There's a saying that courage comes from being afraid and doing it anyway. When you can't summon the motivation or enthusiasm to battle OCD symptoms, put yourself on automatic pilot and go through the motions of behavior therapy anyway. Instead of giving in to your need to wash your hands or check your spelling, do something else for just five minutes.

• Visualize yourself successfully resisting the symptoms of OCD.

• Start small. If you have many rituals, don't try to tackle them all at once. Choose one small thing first—say, refusing to check that the stove is off more than once before leaving the house. When the anxious feelings of OCD tell you to go back again to recheck it, remind yourself that this is your OCD talking.

• Gradually increase the time in which you hold obsessive fears and rituals at bay. If this week you manage five minutes at a time, try to stretch your efforts to ten minutes next week.

• Keep track of each small victory over OCD, and reward yourself for it. Buy yourself something special, see a play, or visit a spa. In time your victories will add up, and you will gain increasing control over your symptoms. This will eventually lead to a more peaceful, happier, healthier, and more productive life in the company of your friends and family.

A FINAL NOTE

Over the course of the last several decades, enormous strides have been made in the diagnosis and treatment of obsessive-compulsive disorder. Astonishingly, it was only thirty years ago that exposure-and-response prevention emerged as the first effective treatment for OCD. Even more amazing, the first effective medications—serotonin-reuptake inhibitors—became available just about ten short years ago.

Before these treatments were discovered and knowledge about OCD gradually became more generally available, people who had this disease were terribly ashamed of their inappropriate thoughts and behavior and went to great lengths to conceal them from family and friends. To some extent that problem still exists today. Although treatment is now available for OCD—the fourth most common psychiatric disorder—not everyone knows about it. Greater education is still necessary.

While much remains to be discovered and accomplished, the coping strategies we have outlined in this chapter and throughout the book can be your path to leading a happier and healthier life in spite of having this troubling disease. As of now no cure exists for obsessive-compulsive disorder, but we do know that we can control OCD symptoms with medication and behavior therapy. In the meantime every day scientists work with state-of-the-art technology to unlock the secrets of OCD. As time goes on, research promises to offer OCD sufferers increasingly more effective solutions and options to live full and productive lives.

Glossary

Addiction A pattern of physical behavior based on an extreme physical and/or psychological need for a substance or activity; different from OCD, as at least at first there is some pleasure in the activity, such as excessive eating or drinking

Agoraphobia An exaggerated fear of leaving the house or other familiar territory

Anafranil A tricyclic antidepressant that, since it has an impact on serotonin, is also prescribed to treat OCD; its generic name is clomipramine

Antidepressant A medication prescribed to relieve depression by changing the function and structure of brain tissue; some antidepressants also help control obsessive-compulsive symptoms

Anxiety Distress, worry, uncertainty, discomfort, and unease; anxiety may be a normal reaction to a real threat, or it may occur unrelated to any particular object or situation due to serotonin abnormalities in OCD

Anxiety disorder A psychological disorder characterized by inappropriate and excessive physical and emotional symptoms of fear, restlessness, rapid heartbeat, and respiration; obsessive-compulsive disorder, generalized anxiety disorder, panic disorder, and phobias are all types of anxiety disorders

Aromatherapy The art of using essential oils distilled from plants, flowers, fruits, and trees to enhance well-being

Attention deficit hyperactivity disorder (ADHD) A mental disorder characterized by limited attention span, restlessness, distractibility, hyperactivity, and compulsiveness

Autism An OCD-related developmental disability that interferes with reasoning, social interaction, and communication skills; common associated problems include obsessive-compulsive behavior, aggression, anxiety, hyperactivity, repetitive body movements, checking, ordering, collecting, and arranging

Basal ganglia Part of the brain fundamentally implicated in OCD

Behavior therapy A form of psychotherapy that focuses on identifying and changing negative patterns of behavior; it differs from cognitive therapy, which centers on changing thought patterns

Benzodiazepines Medications such as Klonopin that are used to treat anxiety disorders

Body dysmorphic disorder (BDD) An OCD-related disorder in which a person believes that his face or body is defective, when to others it appears completely normal

Brain lock UCLA psychiatrist Jeffrey Schwartz's theory that tight and hyperactive linkage among four parts of the brain—the orbital cortex, the caudate nucleus, the cingulate gyrus, and the thalamus—causes the repetitive and intrusive thoughts and habits of OCD

Buspirone A nonaddictive antianxiety drug sometimes added to OCD treatment

Caudate nucleus A part of the basal ganglia in the brain that helps in switching gears from one thought to another; according to current research, the caudate nucleus goes into overdrive along with other parts of the brain to cause OCD symptoms

Checking Repeatedly questioning whether or not you remembered to perform tasks such as locking the door, turning off the stove, or unplugging the iron

Cingulate gyrus A part of the brain that makes your stomach churn and your heart beat faster in response to a threatening situation; according to current research, the cingulate gyrus goes into overdrive along with other parts of the brain to cause OCD symptoms

Clomipramine The generic name for Anafranil

Cognitive therapy A form of psychotherapy that centers on changing thought patterns, especially inaccurate ways in which a person perceives himself and the world

Compulsions An action performed to reduce the distress caused by an obsession

Depression A chronic mood disorder characterized by sleep and appetite changes, sadness, guilt, shame, low self-esteem, anxiety, and extreme fatigue

DSM-IV A shorthand way of referring to the fourth edition of the *Diagnostic and Statistical Manual of Mental Disorders,* the "bible" of mental illness of the American Psychiatric Association, published in 1994

Exposure-and-response prevention A specific type of behavior therapy that involves exposing a person with OCD to whatever usually triggers rituals and helping her to forgo them

Fluoxetine An SSRI antidepressant; the generic name for Prozac

Fluvoxamine An SSRI antidepressant; the generic name for Luvox

Generalized anxiety disorder (GAD) An anxiety disorder characterized by unrealistic and excessive apprehension that lasts for more than six months and interferes with normal functioning

Haloperidol A drug sometimes combined with SSRIs to treat people who have both OCD and Tourette's syndrome

Herbal therapy The use of remedies prepared from roots, leaves, and other parts of plants for healing purposes

Hoarding Collecting and repeatedly counting and stacking useless items

Hypochondriasis An anxiety problem in which one believes one is ill despite all evidence to the contrary

Lithium A mood stabilizer sometimes added to OCD treatment

Luvox An SSRI antidepressant often prescribed to treat OCD; its generic name is fluvoxamine

Monoamine oxidase inhibitor (MAOI) One of a group of antidepressant drugs that works by inhibiting the enzyme monoamine oxidase, which leads to higher levels of norepinephrine, serotonin and dopamine

MRI A diagnostic test using magnetic resonance imaging to monitor brain function; MRIs are safe, sensitive, and noninvasive

Neurons Nerve cells, the basic units of the nervous system

Neurotransmitter A special chemical released by neurons in the brain to carry messages about moods and emotions across synapses

Norepinephrine A type of neurotransmitter that helps to regulate moods

Obsession An unsettling and distressing thought or image that is virtually impossible to control

Obsessional slowness An absorption in completing in exact order every aspect of a time-consuming ritual

Obsessive-compulsive personality disorder A condition involving a general preoccupation with orderliness, perfectionism, and control; sometimes mistakenly confused with OCD, but it is not characterized by obsessions and compulsions

Orbital cortex A part of the brain that may be implicated in OCD; according to current research, the orbital cortex goes into overdrive along with other parts of the brain to cause OCD symptoms

PANDAS The acronym for children who have pediatric autoimmune neuropsychiatric disorders associated with streptococcal infections

Panic attack An episode of sudden, unprovoked, and intense anxiety, fear, and discomfort; physical symptoms include a rapid heartbeat, dizziness, nausea, shortness of breath, and general loss of control

Paroxetine An SSRI antidepressant; the generic name for Paxil

Paxil An SSRI antidepressant often prescribed to treat OCD; its generic name is paroxetine

PET scan A diagnostic test using positron-emission tomography, a type of brain imaging, to monitor brain function

Phobias Exaggerated and often disabling fears of objects or situations unrelated to any realistic danger; a specific phobia is a fear of a particular object or situation, while a social phobia is a more generalized fear of being painfully embarrassed in social situations

Pimozide A drug sometimes combined with an SSRI to treat people who have both OCD and Tourette's syndrome

Prozac An SSRI antidepressant often prescribed to treat OCD; its generic name is fluoxetine

Psychiatrist A physician specializing in disorders of the mind; in contrast to psychologists, psychiatrists are medical doctors who can write prescriptions

Psychologist A therapist with a doctoral degree in psychology that may include training in counseling, psychotherapy, and psychological testing

Psychotherapy Psychological treatment that involves talking with a therapist to understand and resolve conflicts

Pure obsessions Disturbing thoughts that do not have any corresponding rituals

Receptor A special chemical on the surface of a neuron that receives neurotransmitters

Reuptake Reabsorption of a neurotransmitter by the neuron that released it

Selective serotonin-reuptake inhibitor (SSRI) One of a group of antidepressant drugs that work by selectively preventing the reuptake of the neurotransmitter serotonin; they ordinarily do not affect other neurotransmitters

Serotonin A type of neurotransmitter that helps to regulate mood and is specifically implicated in obsessive-compulsive disorder

Serotonin syndrome An accumulation of too much serotonin that can cause agitation, confusion, tremors, and muscle spasms

Sertraline An SSRI antidepressant; the generic name for Zoloft

Side effect An unintended response that accompanies the intended effect of a medication

Stress Anything that causes an action or reaction in the body, emotional or physical, positive or negative

Superstition A belief that an object, action, or circumstance will influence the outcome of an unrelated event

Synapse A tiny, fluid-filled gap between nerve cells, through which messages are carried by neurotransmitters

Thalamus A part of the brain that processes signals from the cortex and other areas; according to current research, the thalamus goes into overdrive along with other parts of the brain to cause obsessive-compulsive symptoms

Tic A sudden and involuntary repeated movement or vocalization. Tics include sounds such as snorting, sniffing, mumbling, stuttering, grunting, barking, or coughing. Motor tics may include touching, squatting, deep knee bends, hopping, skipping, and twirling or retracing steps while walking

Tourette's syndrome A severe type of OCD-related tic disorder that first appears before the age of eighteen

Trichotillomania An OCD-related disorder, more common in women than men, in which there is an urge to compulsively pull out scalp hair, eyelashes, eyebrows, and pubic hair

Tricyclic antidepressant One of a group of antidepressant medications named for their chemical structure, which includes three rings of carbon atoms

Tryptophan An amino acid that is a precursor of serotonin and is sometimes added to OCD treatment

Undoing ritual A compulsion, such as repeating certain phrases or counting backward from one thousand, to ward off a disaster hinted at by an obsession

Washout A period of time to allow one medication to leave your body before your psychiatrist switches you to another

Zoloft An SSRI antidepressant often prescribed to treat OCD; its generic name is sertraline

Appendix A

Further Resources

The Obsessive-Compulsive Foundation (OCF)
P.O. Box 70
Milford, CT 06460
phone: (203) 878–5669

Obsessive-Compulsive Anonymous (OCA)
P.O. Box 215
New Hyde Park, NY 11040
phone: (516) 741–4901

American Psychiatric Association
1400 K Street, N.W.
Washington, DC 20005
phone: (202) 682–6325
fax: (202) 682–6255

American Psychological Association
750 First Street, N.E.
Washington, DC 20002–4242
phone: (202) 336–5500

The American Self-Help Clearinghouse
St. Clares-Riverside Medical Center
Denville, NJ 07034
phone: (973) 625–7101

Anxiety Disorders Association of America
(ADAA)
6000 Executive Boulevard
Rockville, MD 20852–3801
phone: (301) 231–9350

The Association for Advancement of Behavior
Therapy (AABT)
15 West 36th Street
New York, NY 10018

Autism Society of America (ASA)
7910 Woodmont Avenue, Suite 650
Bethesda, MD 20814
phone: (800) 3–AUTISM
Web site: http://www.autism-society.org

National Institute of Mental Health (NIMH)
5600 Fishers Lane
Rockville, MD 20857
phone: (301) 443–4513

National Mental Health Association
1021 Prince Street
Alexandria, VA 22314
phone: (703) 684–7722 or (800) 969–NMHA

Appendix B

Further Reading

American Psychiatric Association *Diagnostic and Statistical Manual of Mental Disorders Fourth Edition* (Washington, D.C.: American Psychiatric Press, 1994)

Baer, Lee, Ph.D. *Getting Control: Overcoming Your Obsessions and Compulsions* (Boston: Little, Brown & Co., 1991)

Dumont, Reann. *The Sky Is Falling: Understanding and Coping With Phobias, Panic, and Obsessive-Compulsive Disorders* (New York: W.W. Norton, 1996)

Grandin, Temple. *Thinking in Pictures: And Other Reports from My Life with Autism* (New York: Doubleday, 1995)

Matisik, Edward N., M.A. *The Americans With Disabilities Act and the Rehabilitation Act of 1973: Reasonable Accommodations for Employees with OCD* (New Milford, CT: OC Foundation booklet, 1996)

Neziroglu, Fugen, Ph.D., and Jose A. Yaryura-Tobias, M.D. *Over and Over Again* (New York: Lexington Books, 1991)

Rapoport, Judith L., M.D. *The Boy Who Couldn't Stop Washing* (New York: Signet, 1991)

Sacks, Oliver, M.D. *Awakenings* (New York: Dutton, 1983)

Schwartz, Jeffrey M., M.D. *Brain Lock: Free Yourself From Obsessive-Compulsive Behavior* (New York: Harper Collins, 1996)

Steketee, Gail, Ph.D. and Kerrin White, M.D. *When Once Is Not Enough* (Oakland, California: New Harbinger Publications, 1990)

Index